WHEN LIFE DOESN'T GO YOUR WAY

HOPE FOR CATHOLIC WOMEN FACING
DISAPPOINTMENT AND PAIN

KATRINA J. ZENO

theWORD
among us®
press

Published by The Word Among Us Press
9639 Doctor Perry Road
Ijamsville, Maryland 21754
www.wordamongus.org

14 13 12 11 10   2 3 4 5 6
ISBN: 978-1-59325-152-9

Cover design by The DesignWorks Group

Made and printed in the United States of America
Library of Congress Cataloging-in-Publication Data

Zeno, Katrina J.
  When life doesn't go your way : hope for Catholic women facing disappointment and pain / Katrina J. Zeno.
      p. cm.
  ISBN 978-1-59325-152-9 (alk. paper)
  1. Catholic women--Religious life. 2. Pain--Religious aspects--Catholic Church. 3. Disappointment--Religious aspescts--Catholic Church. 4. Suffering--Religious aspescts--Catholic Church. I. Title.
  BX2353.Z46 2009
  248.8'6--dc22
                                                        2009000096

This book is dedicated to all the women
who have shared their brokenness with me.

Contents

Introduction   6

1. The Goodness of God   8

2. The Script Changes . . . Unexpectedly   25

3. The Way of the Cross   45

4. The Eucharistic Pattern   62

5. The Divine Marinade   97

6. The Body, Suffering, and Love   129

7. A Final Cup of Tea   149

Sources and Acknowledgments   153

INTRODUCTION

W hy?"

It's a question we all ask. We want to know why things happen. We want to grasp the meaning and purpose behind what we're experiencing, the suffering we're enduring, or the choice someone else makes that directly affects us. Sometimes the answers are clear; more often they require an act of faith like my experience of Banff, Canada. I was told that the quaint village was surrounded by mountains, but I couldn't see them. The clouds were so thick the one and only morning I visited that to this day, I have to believe by faith (not by sight) that they truly were there.

In our own lives, most of us have a mental "script" of how we think life will go. And, of course, that script has a happy ending. However, that's not always what happens. Infants die. Teenage girls become pregnant. Alcoholism turns ugly. Buildings blow up. Heart attacks whisk loved ones away. Colliding with a sudden script change can push us to one extreme or the other. On the one hand, it can shatter our faith, especially when we can't see the mountains, and the pain screams to be numbed through a glass of alcohol or a glorious chocolate binge. On the other hand, unexpected life changes can invite us to press deeper into God.

Why does the script of life change? Why doesn't life go the way we want? Is there a meaning and purpose behind these events? Can we hold onto faith, even when we can't see the outcome? Can we believe in a good God, despite crushing tragedy and suffering?

Faith, joy, and happiness rise and fall on these questions. There is no shame in asking why. It's the most human thing to do. The challenge is to keep asking why until the light of faith pierces the clouds. Until then, may we say with the centurion who sought Jesus' healing power, "I do believe, help my unbelief!" (Mark 9:24).

CHAPTER 1

THE GOODNESS OF GOD

God is good . . . all the time.

How do you feel when you read that sentence? Is your heart leaping for joy and enthusiasm? Or do you want to throw this book against the wall or flush it down the toilet? If you're currently suffering a trial or disappointment, or know someone who is, my suspicion is that you might opt for the latter. It may be difficult to believe that God is good . . . all the time.

In the midst of a world where bad things happen to good people, our faith in the goodness of God can falter. In fact, our faith in God's existence can falter. Just last week a wheelchair-bound mother with multiple sclerosis told me how her twenty-year-old son said to her, "How can you believe in a God who would allow this to happen to you?"

His question is honest and haunting.

The tragedy of evil, pain, and suffering is its ability to disconnect us from God, to make God feel distant, far away, and coldly uninvolved in our lives and our suffering. However, God's greatest desire is just the opposite: to be connected to us, to be actively involved in our lives. God wants to communicate his goodness to us, even when life doesn't go our way and the future is uncertain.

If God is good all the time, then what does this goodness look like? I once read a story about a young new pastor and his wife who were assigned to reopen a run-down, inner-city church. The story appeared in a 1954 edition of *Reader's Digest*. Here's a summarized version:

Once long ago an old church had flourished, but now the good days had passed from that section of town. However, the pastor and his young wife believed in their run-down church. They felt that with paint, hammer, and faith, they could get it in shape. Together they went to work.

Late in December a severe storm whipped through the river valley, and a huge chunk of rain-soaked plaster fell out of the inside wall of the church just behind the altar. Sorrowfully the pastor and his wife swept away the mess, but they couldn't hide the ragged hole. And Christmas was only two days away.

That afternoon the dispirited couple attended a benefit auction. One of the items was a handsome gold and ivory lace tablecloth, nearly fifteen feet long. The pastor was seized with what he thought was a great idea. He won the bid for $6.50. Delighted, the pastor carried the cloth back to the church and tacked it up on the wall behind the altar. It completely hid the hole! Happily he went back to preparing his Christmas sermon.

Just before noon on Christmas Eve, as the pastor was opening the church, he noticed a woman standing in the cold at the bus stop. "The bus won't be here for forty minutes!" he called, and invited her into the church to get warm.

She told him that she had come from the city that morning to be interviewed for a job as governess to the children of one of the wealthy families in town, but she had been turned down. A war refugee, her English was imperfect.

The woman sat down in a pew and rested. She looked up as the pastor began to adjust the great gold and ivory cloth across the hole. She rose suddenly and walked up toward him, looking at the tablecloth. The pastor smiled and started to tell her about the storm damage, but she didn't seem to listen. She took up a fold of the cloth and rubbed it between her fingers.

"It's mine!" she said. "It's my banquet cloth!" She lifted up a corner and showed the surprised pastor that her initials were monogrammed on it. "My husband had the cloth made especially for me in Brussels! There could not be another like it."

For the next few minutes the woman and the pastor talked excitedly together. She explained that she was Viennese; she and her husband had opposed the Nazis and decided to leave the country. Her husband put her on a train for Switzerland, and they planned that he would join her as soon as he could ship their household goods across the border. She never saw him again. Later she heard that he had died in a concentration camp.

"I have always felt that it was my fault—to leave without him," she said. "Perhaps these years of wandering have been my punishment." The pastor tried to comfort her and urged her to take the cloth with her. She refused. Then she left.

As the church began to fill on Christmas Eve, it was clear that the cloth was going to be a great success. It had been skillfully designed to look its best by candlelight.

After the service, the pastor stood at the doorway. Many people told him that the church looked beautiful. One middle-aged man, the local clock and watch repairman, looked rather puzzled.

"It is strange," he said in his soft accent. "Many years ago my wife—God rest her—and I owned such a cloth. In our home in Vienna, my wife put it on the table"—and here he smiled—"only when the bishop came to dinner."

The pastor suddenly became very excited. He told the jeweler about the woman who had been in church earlier that day. The startled jeweler clutched the pastor's arm. "Can it be? Is she alive?"

Together the two got in touch with the family who had interviewed her. Then, in the pastor's car they started for the city. And as Christmas Day was born, this man and his wife, who had been separated through so many Christmases, were reunited.[1]

The husband and wife had been disconnected for many years, but the tablecloth brought them back together. The goodness of God reconnected them; he brought them into the warmth and presence of each other through the "apparent" tragedy of a severe storm.

God wants to do the same thing for you—to reconnect you to himself, to bring you into his presence and warmth, whether it's been a couple of days or a couple of decades since you've felt that connection. God wants you to know, beyond the shadow of a doubt, that *he exists, and that he cares for you personally*—like the couple and the tablecloth—even when the storms in life seem to create gaping holes instead of wonderful reunions.

A Second Touch

The Gospel of Mark tells the story of a blind man who needed to experience the goodness of God, who needed to know that God cared for him personally, even in the midst of blanketing darkness (8:22-25). Some friends bring the man to Jesus and beg Jesus to touch him. Jesus touches the man's eyes, but when the man first opens them, his vision is fuzzy. People look like trees. Only when Jesus lays his hands on the man's eyes a second time is his sight perfectly restored.

This man's experience may be a reflection of our own. Perhaps in the past you felt a touch of the Master's hand, you felt connected to God, but now you need a second touch; you need to know *again* that God is good (all the time) and that he cares for you personally. You need Christ to come along and touch the ragged hole in your heart and reconnect you with God.

St. Paul is another marvelous example of someone who became reconnected to God. In the Book of Acts, his name is Saul, and he's on a mission—to destroy the infant Church and all those who follow Jesus on "the way." However, on Saul's way to Damascus, a light suddenly flashes around him, and a voice says, "Saul, Saul, why are you persecuting me?" Saul asks, "Who are you, sir?" and the voice answers, "I am Jesus, whom you are persecuting" (see Acts 9:4-5).

Saul gets up, the Bible tells us, but when "he opened his eyes he could see nothing" (Acts 9:8). It wasn't until three days later, when Ananias prays for Saul and something like scales fall from his eyes that he can see. He can now see with the eyes of faith, not just with human eyes, and his life is never the same.

How do we learn to see with the eyes of faith? It's not always easy, but when we hear stories about others who have seen with the eyes of faith, it builds up our own faith.

A friend of mine named Patty experienced desperate financial difficulty early in her marriage. One day she needed milk and toilet paper, but she only had enough money to buy one or the other. At the store, she stood debating about which one to buy. Finally, she decided on the milk.

That night she and her family were awakened by a noise outside their home, and they went to the front door just in time to see a car speeding away. And what to their wondering eyes should appear? Their trees were completely covered with toilet paper, and there were four rolls sitting on their porch. Someone had toilet papered the wrong house! When they told the story to a friend, the friend said, "Thank goodness you bought the milk—otherwise you might have found a cow on your porch!"

Even in the midst of financial desperation, Patty saw those toilet-papered trees with the eyes of faith. She experienced God's goodness—that he exists and cares for her personally—and it's an experience she's never forgotten.

In our own lives, God wants to give us the eyes of faith, especially when it comes to our personal history and our understanding of the Bible. Instead of seeing the Bible as a tedious description of this person begetting that person or this nation fighting that nation, we can see God's story—and *our* story woven into his. Bible scholar Dr. Scott Hahn has a marvelous ability to see Scripture with the eyes of faith: he sees the story of God extending his covenant love from one holy couple (Adam and Eve) to one holy family (Noah) to one holy tribe (Abraham) to one holy nation (Israel) to one holy kingdom (David) to one holy people (the Church).

GOD'S LOVE IS INCLUSIVE

When we see God's story in Scripture with the eyes of faith, we learn that God's love is not exclusive but inclusive. *No one is excluded from the Father's love.* This was hard for St. Paul to get at first, but when he got it, he really got it! Here's how he described this truth in Ephesians 1:3-5: "Blessed be the God and Father of our Lord Jesus Christ, who has blessed us in Christ with every spiritual blessing in the heavens, as he chose us in him, before the foundation of the world, to be holy and without blemish before him. In love he destined us for adoption to himself through Jesus Christ, in accord with the favor of his will. . . ."

St. Paul got it! Even before God created the world, he had a plan—and that plan was to bring everyone into his family as his adopted sons and daughters. He chose you, in Christ, before the world began, to be part of his family. His one desire from all eternity has been to be connected to you through his family.

I have a number of friends who have adopted children, and one thing I've noticed is that it's never an easy process. Some dear friends named Ann and Sam had been married about fifteen years and were unable to have children. Finally, through an adoption agency in the United States, they got word of a young single woman in Texas who was pregnant and planning to give up her baby for adoption.

They were so excited. They started the legal and financial process to pay for the adoption. Ann quit her job, and they moved to a larger house in anticipation of starting their family. Then they got the news: after giving birth, the woman and her child disappeared and couldn't be found. My friends were crushed.

Then I received an e-mail message from Ann, who was writing from Lebanon. Her husband, Sam, is Lebanese American, and they had really wanted to adopt from Lebanon. However, adoption is highly discouraged in that culture because the extended family is expected to care for a child rather than release the baby for adoption. As a result, Ann and Sam had hit wall after wall whenever they had tried to pursue adoption in that country. Suddenly they were in Lebanon with their newborn adopted daughter, asking for prayers for the paperwork to be completed so they could bring her home. After four months, Ann and Sam returned home with their darling Lebanese daughter. Ann and Sam went through great effort, heartache, and financial cost to adopt their daughter, but I can tell you, it was worth it!

BAPTISMAL ADOPTION

God the Father has done the same with you. He's gone through great effort, heartache, and the cost of the cross to adopt you into his family, but it was so worth it! You are so worth it to God that he would have sent his Son even if you were the only person on earth, because he chose *you*, in Christ, before the world began.

Ann and Sam traveled from the United States to Lebanon to adopt their daughter and had to wait four months to get her passport before they could bring her home. Jesus Christ traveled a much greater distance; he traveled the infinite distance from heaven to earth to become one of us so that you could be adopted into the family of God. And he's given you not an earthly passport but a spiritual passport, a passport to heaven. And he's done this through your baptism.

Sometimes I think it's easy to forget how utterly earthshaking baptism is, how it really changes us from being spiritual orphans to being part of the family of God. After the scales fell from Saul's eyes, he immediately wanted to be baptized. During his time of physical blindness, God opened the eyes of his heart to see the goodness of God through baptism—the baptism that reconnects us to God, to the Trinity, and makes every person, whether Jew or Gentile, part of the family of God.

At your baptism, God marked you with an indelible seal, what the Church calls your baptismal character. This is your spiritual passport, and it doesn't say "American" or "Italian" or "German"—it says "Christian." You belong to Christ. You belong to God. His blood runs through your veins.

History is, indeed, his story, but it's also *your* story—the story of God's choosing one holy couple, one holy family, one holy tribe, one holy nation, one holy kingdom, and one holy people so that he could adopt you into the family of God through your baptism.

God Cares for Us

Baptism is just the beginning of being reconnected to God, of experiencing the goodness of God in our lives. God wants us to experience his goodness throughout our lives—to have the eyes of faith as a young adult, a middle-aged adult, and a close-to-glory adult—so that our permanent memory bank knows that God exists and that he cares for us personally.

How does God care for us personally? Here's one small example. When my son Michael was sixteen, he and his basketball team had just finished practice at a public-school gym, and I'd come to pick him up. A couple of the kids were still waiting for their parents, so we waited with them. As we were waiting, another one of the kids called my son on his cell phone and asked him to go back into the gym and pick up a shirt he forgot. We tried the front doors, but they were locked. We went around to the back doors, and fortunately they were still open. My son popped into the gym, reappeared a minute later, sat down next to me in the car, and said, "God works in mysterious ways." The maternal catechist in me was surprised (and delighted!) at his simple confession of faith. Michael went on to explain how, as he walked into the gym, he saw his wallet lying on the floor. It had evidently fallen out of his pants, and he didn't know it. The forgotten shirt had reconnected him with his prodigal wallet!

God is good . . . all the time. My son saw the goodness of God with the eyes of faith, and he experienced God's personal care for him through a forgotten shirt and a found wallet.

Pastor Sam Roetzer also experienced the goodness of God in a dramatic way. Sam met his wife in high school, and they dated for five years. The Vietnam War was in full swing, and after graduation, Sam knew he would be drafted. He decided to enlist in the army, and within a short time he got his papers to go to Vietnam. He and his girlfriend, who was now his fiancée, had planned to get married on December 30. He suggested postponing the wedding until after he returned. She said no. They got married on December 30, and he left for Vietnam on February 3.

As soon as he landed in Vietnam and got off the plane, Sam had a stark reality check: sitting on the tarmac was a row of body bags waiting to be loaded on his plane. He swallowed hard and kept walking. At the army camp, he was assigned to the local supply unit. His job was to drive to the main supply unit to get gas and flight fuel. "This will be a piece of cake," he thought. However, the main supply unit was in a rural area far away, and the road was so narrow that when two trucks met, their side-view mirrors clicked in passing. Moreover, the truck he would be driving held not fifty, but five thousand gallons of gas, thus making it a traveling explosive.

For the first twelve days, he drove as a passenger with his sergeant. Then, on the thirteenth day, his sergeant told him he was ready to go solo. At age twenty, Sam climbed into the huge truck and started off down the road alone. Less than two miles later, two gunshots pierced the passenger side of the windshield. It scared the daylights out of him. For the first time in thirteen days, he prayed. "God, be with me. Come and be beside me." He made it to the main supply unit, filled up the tank, and headed back.

When he arrived back at his own supply unit and the sergeant saw the two bullet holes on the passenger side, he said, "Son,

Someone was with you today. I wasn't sure why I told you to go by yourself, but now I know why." (Civilian translation: If the sergeant had been driving and Sam had been in the passenger seat, Sam would have been dead.)

For thirteen months, Sam drove that truck back and forth, and every time he asked Jesus to come and sit beside him. Sam had his eyes opened that day to the goodness of God. He knew that God existed and that he cared for him personally.

Blessed Mother Teresa of Calcutta also knew the goodness of God. She knew God's personal care for her, even in the midst of abject poverty and disease. She had the eyes of faith to see the goodness of God, to see God's love and care for each person, no matter how sick, poor, or physically disabled he or she might be. One day Mother Teresa was begging on the streets of Calcutta for her ministry, and a well-dressed businessman came along and spit on her hand. Mother Teresa wiped her hand off and said, "That was for me." Then she stuck her hand out again and said, "Now do you have something for the poor?" Even though he spit on her hand, she didn't react in anger. She knew her dignity came from God's love and care for her. And so she continued to ask for money for her ministry from this man who had insulted her.

I want to be like Mother Teresa, Sam, and Patty. I want to be able to see the goodness of God all around me. I want to have the eyes of faith to know that God exists and that he cares for me personally.

BEAUTY'S PURPOSE

The first time I visited Phoenix, Arizona, I spent several days north of the city at a friend's house, which is halfway up a mountain. Sitting on her back veranda, one can see the expansive valley below. One evening at sunset, we watched as row upon row of mountains turned pink and then purple and then mauve. I was awed at the beauty of God's creation because, living in Steubenville, Ohio, I didn't have many opportunities to see natural beauty.

As I reflected on this experience, it struck me: the purpose of beauty is to make us stop—stop what we are doing; stop rushing around; stop, look, and see the goodness of God and reconnect with him.

I once heard a story about a monk who, along with two young novices, was waiting outside an office building in New York City one summer day. A beautiful woman walked by, and since it was summer, she was dressed for the hot weather. The abbot continued to watch the woman until finally one of the young novices said, "Ahem. Brother Abbot, you're embarrassing us." And the abbot asked, "Why?" The novice replied, "Well, you know, the way you keep looking at her."

"Oh," the abbot said, "I was thinking about how beautiful she is and how beautiful God must be to create such beauty and how beautiful she must be on the inside, and I was praying for her." Beauty made the abbot stop, look, and think of the goodness and beauty of God.

Wouldn't it be great if beauty could do the same for us? When we see a starry night, we could take the time to stop and think, "God is good . . . all the time." When we see a hummingbird in flight, we could allow this encounter to reconnect us with God. When we see a beautiful woman, we could say to ourselves, "I know that God exists; how else could such beauty come about?"

I'd like you to close your eyes for a minute and imagine in your mind something that makes you stop and notice and reconnect with God. Maybe it's a beautiful rose, or a tiny newborn baby, or a soft white blanket of new-fallen snow. Maybe it's a beautiful piece of music or the sight of an elderly person, hunched over and shuffling along. These are God's fingerprints, the tracks that he's left behind on earth; tracks that we're meant to follow to lead us to God; tracks that open our eyes to see beyond what's immediately visible.

St. Augustine once said, "Our whole business, therefore, in this life is to restore to health the eye of the heart whereby God may be seen."[2] Isn't that our life business as well—to believe in the goodness of God until the eye of our heart can see it?

GOD WANTS TO OPEN OUR EYES

I'd like to end this chapter with a story about the prophet Elisha and the "eye of the heart" that is capable of seeing beyond what's immediately visible.

Here's the situation in the Second Book of Kings, chapter 6: The king of Aram is on the warpath against Israel, but every time he's ready to attack, his plan is foiled. Eventually, he discovers why—God is revealing to the prophet Elisha the king's plans and alerting Israel to his strategy. Needless to say, the king is steaming mad. He finds out that Elisha is staying in the city of Dothan and resolves to kill him. The king surrounds the city at night with a strong force of horses and chariots. The next morning, Elisha's servant gets up to get his cappuccino and paper, and sees the enemy army and panics. He runs to Elisha and says, "What shall we do? What shall we do?"

Elisha calmly answers, "Do not be afraid. Our side outnumbers theirs" (2 Kings 6:16). His servant is convinced that Elisha has gone off his rocker. But then Elisha prays, "'O LORD, open his eyes, that he may see.' And the LORD opened the eyes of the servant, so that he saw the mountainside filled with horses and fiery chariots around Elisha" (6:17).

The servant's eyes were opened, and he could see the goodness of God; he could see with the eyes of faith beyond what was immediately evident.

God wants to open our eyes; he wants to give us the eyes of faith so that we can see the goodness of God in our baptism, in trees full of toilet paper, in lost wallets, and in the beauty around us that makes us stop, look, and say, "God is good . . . all the time. He exists, and he cares for me personally." I encourage you to take a moment and thank God for all the times in your life when you have experienced his goodness, and to pray for the eyes of faith to see the invisible through the visible.

Questions for Reflection and Discussion

1. Can you share a time when you have experienced the goodness of God?

2. Why do you think it's difficult for some people to believe that God is good . . . all the time?

3. What is something that makes you stop and notice and reconnect with God?

4. At this moment, do you need a second touch of the Master's hand to be reconnected with God, or are you feeling closely connected?

5. Why do you think St. Paul wanted to be baptized? What does baptism mean to you?

6. Take a moment to pray, and ask God to open the eye of your heart to see God in the circumstances around you.

CHAPTER 2

THE SCRIPT CHANGES . . .
UNEXPECTEDLY

I love to laugh. Laughing not only lifts the corners of my mouth, but it also floods my brain with uplifting endorphins. Momentarily I no longer feel like Atlas, carrying the world on my shoulders. Even though this chapter discusses an immensely serious subject, I hope you won't mind if I begin with some load-lightening stories. Here they are:

A woman invited some people to her home for dinner. At the table, she turned to her six-year-old daughter and said, "Would you like to say the blessing?"

"I wouldn't know what to say," the little girl replied.

"Just say what you hear Mommy say," her mother answered.

The daughter bowed her head and said, "Lord, why on earth did I invite all these people to dinner?"[1]

A mother was teaching her three-year-old the Our Father. For several months at bedtime, the child repeated it after the mother. Then one night the child was ready to go solo. The mother listened with pride to the carefully enunciated words, right up to the end, when she prayed: "And lead us not into temptation, but deliver us some e-mail."[2]

And finally, the last humorous story:

A four-year-old girl was at the pediatrician's office for a checkup. As the doctor looked into her ears, he asked, "Do you think I'll find Big Bird in here?" The little girl didn't say anything. Next, he took the tongue depressor and looked down her throat, asking, "Do you think I'll find Cookie Monster down there?" Again the little girl was silent. Then the doctor put a stethoscope to her chest. As he listened to her heart beat, he asked, "Do you think I'll find Barney in there?" "Oh no!" the little girl replied. "Jesus is in my heart. Barney's on my underpants."[3]

Have you ever thought about why we laugh at jokes? It's because the outcome is unexpected. We don't expect the little girl to say Jesus is in her heart and Barney is on her underpants. It's not the script we expected to hear, nor the category we usually think in.

Jesus was a master at understanding how people thought and the categories they used to make sense out of the world and their experiences. Jesus "did not need anyone to testify about human nature. He himself understood it well" (John 2:25). But he was also a master at inviting people to change their categories of thinking.

The Gospel of Mark provides numerous situations in which Jesus invites those around him to change their thinking. In one incident in chapter 2, four men bring a paralytic man to Jesus by letting him down through the roof. They're expecting Jesus to heal him physically. But instead, Jesus says, "Child, your sins are forgiven" (2:5). Jesus heals him spiritually, and the Jews go berserk because only God can forgive sins. For Jesus to forgive the man's sins was absolutely contrary to the categories that the Jews were used to thinking in. Through his actions, Jesus is saying: "God forgives sin. I'm forgiving sin. Therefore, I am God. Change your categories of thinking."

A little later in the same chapter, some Jews come to Jesus and essentially say: "Good Jews fast. The Pharisees fast. The disciples of John the Baptist fast. How come your disciples don't fast?" And Jesus answers, "Can the wedding guests fast while the bridegroom is with them?" (Mark 2:19). In short, he's saying, "My disciples aren't fasting because I am no ordinary man. I am the Bridegroom among you. Change your categories of thinking."

And finally, there's the man with the withered hand in Mark 3. In the Jewish mind, the category of the Sabbath went something like this: "God rested on the seventh day. God commanded us to honor the Sabbath and keep it holy. Therefore, no good Jew works on the Sabbath." Jesus shows up at the synagogue and asks, "Is it lawful to do good on the sabbath rather than to do evil, to save life rather than to destroy it?" (3:4). When he gets no answer, Jesus tells the man to stretch out his hand, and it is healed. And Mark says the Pharisees closed their minds to him and immediately began to plot how to kill Jesus (see 3:6). They couldn't change their categories of thinking.

Changing Our Categories of Thinking

In order to make sense out of the script changes of life, we frequently have to follow this same pattern: we need to change our categories of thinking. This is particularly true when it comes to prayer. I'm suspicious that many of us, including me, have absorbed the thought that the purpose of prayer is to get our prayers answered: we have a need, we go to God, and we pray. Although bringing our petitions and intercessions before God is a good and noble form of prayer, it's not the primary purpose of prayer. The primary purpose of prayer is not to get our prayers answered but to grow in a deeper relationship with God. I'd like to emphasize that again: the primary purpose of prayer is to grow closer to God, to press into him.

When I go to sleep at night, I have a nifty pillow made out of special foam. When I lay my head on it, when I press into it, it molds around me. That's similar to prayer—we press into God, and he molds his intimate presence around us.

What I've noticed over the years is that, whether we realize it or not, we all have a script of life we're writing in our heads that fits neatly into our categories of thinking. We think life will go a certain way. (I'll grow up, get married, have four or five children, live to a happy old age.) We think people and our children will act a certain way. (My boss will be nice to me. My children will obey me. I'll meet a cute, handsome guy on CatholicMatch.com, and he'll fall madly in love with me. My in-laws will love me.) We think God will act a certain way. (He'll answer my prayers. He'll bless me spiritually and materially. He'll protect me from all harm and evil.)

But then life doesn't always go the way we may have expected. We're still single at thirty-five or we become single again at fifty-five. Our children make choices that cause us pain and suffering. Our job doesn't provide the satisfaction we thought it would. We experience infertility or miscarriage. A loved one unexpectedly develops cancer and dies, or we develop cancer and are facing surgery and possibly death.

Have you ever noticed that one of our faults as humans, particularly those of us of the feminine persuasion, is that we compare ourselves to each other? We look at others and think: "She got the life she signed up for. She has the perfect husband. Her kids are wonderful. I'm sure she never feels lonely, isolated, or ugly. She always looks so cheerful and full of energy. She's got it all together."

You know what? *She* doesn't exist. If you scratch beneath the surface, you'll find that for most women (and men), there were dreams that died and losses they never expected to face.

The bottom line is that life doesn't go the way we expected, and we're not laughing. On the contrary, we can sometimes be like the Israelites in the desert who grumbled and complained and said, "Would that we had died at the LORD's hand in the land of Egypt, as we sat by our fleshpots and ate our fill of bread! But you had to lead us into this desert to make the whole community die of famine!" (Exodus 16:3).

STORIES OF SCRIPT CHANGES

At times like this, it's easy to question God's goodness: "If you're a good God, how could you allow this to happen?" "I did everything a good parent was supposed to do. How could you allow my son to get involved with the wrong crowd or my daughter to become pregnant?" "How could you allow alcoholism to rip my family apart?" "How could you allow this relationship to end?" "I've gone to church every Sunday. I've followed all the rules. How could you allow us to lose our home?" Instead of taking us deeper into prayer, pain and suffering can take us deeper into hurt. Instead of pressing deeper into God, we're tempted to walk away from God.

I'd like to relate some more stories, but these aren't jokes. These are real stories of real people who experienced life not going the way they wanted. Instead of turning away from God, they allowed the script change to turn them toward God, to press them into God, to reconnect them with God. After much struggle and even combating with God, they changed their categories of thinking and walked through the doorway of surrender to deeper prayer, intimacy, and peace.

Belize Bride. Many summers ago, I heard a man share about his life in a matchbox-sized village in Belize (population: fifty). One day when he was a young man, he walked to the neighboring town. There he noticed a very beautiful woman. He made it a point to meet her, and he began visiting her as often as he could, even though she lived almost two hours away. For a year he made the long trek to her family's home whenever he could, and eventually he began building his own home. Finally, he made the two-hour trip, nervous and excited because he felt the day had come to ask her to marry him.

He arrived at the woman's house and was met by her mother, who began chatting with him. And chatting. And chatting. Fifteen minutes, twenty minutes, a half hour, forty-five minutes went by. Finally, he asked the mother where his soon-to-be bride was. There was a brief silence, and then the mother replied that she had gotten married the day before.

Can you imagine how crushed this man felt? In fact, as he traveled home, thoughts of suicide filled his mind. What is the purpose of living? Is there a God? If so, how could he let this happen? He started asking questions, and instead of finding immediate answers, he found something much better: he found God.

The reason I heard this story is because the man who told it included it as part of his homily. He became a priest. The agony in his heart led him to pray, to dialogue with God, to turn toward God and press into God, which led him to the priesthood.

Imagine how different this man's life would have been if he had married the very beautiful woman. Instead, God used the changed script to call him into the priesthood. The man changed his categories of thinking and married another beautiful Bride. Pain and suffering jump-started his relationship with God and redirected his path in a totally unexpected but fulfilling way.

LESLIE'S FAMILY. There's a woman I know named Leslie, who graduated from college, worked as a nanny in France, and was still single at the age of twenty-seven. Obviously, it's not the end of the world to be single at twenty-seven, but if you were planning to be married and have children by age twenty-three, sometimes it can feel as if you missed God's plan.

However, in God's providence, Leslie met a handsome concert pianist, and wedding bells soon chimed. Within a year, a son was born and seventeen months later, another son. Baby paraphernalia, diapers, and first smiles reawakened her original expectation for many children. Then Leslie experienced a miscarriage, and another, and a third in which she almost bled to death.

Suddenly the script changed. Instead of having half a dozen children, Leslie and her husband had to avoid pregnancy just so that she didn't die.

To the outside world, Leslie's life looked ideal. She had a beautiful brick home, two healthy, handsome boys, and a loving, talented husband. On the inside, Leslie had to adjust to a changed script, to the forced downsizing of her family and to the loss of children she would never have.

Then at Mass one morning, I noticed that Leslie was carrying a wrapped-up bundle. I thought to myself, "I know I haven't seen her in a couple of months, but could she possibly have been pregnant and given birth?" I quickly discovered that wasn't the case. Instead, someone who knew that Leslie and her husband wanted more children contacted them and said they knew of a young woman who was pregnant and was intending to give her baby up for adoption. Would they be interested? Of course! So here was Leslie, the proud mom of a tiny infant daughter. And here's how God works to tailor the details. Leslie has dark skin because she is part Trinidadian, and her husband is Maltese, so he has an olive complexion. Their daughter is biracial, so she fits right into the family with dark skin and hair, just like Leslie, her husband, and two sons.

But the story isn't over. Leslie became pregnant again and delivered a full-term baby girl, whom they named Anastasia. And she had Down syndrome, with two enormous holes in the upper and lower chambers of her heart. As a result, Anastasia was constantly close to heart failure.

When Anastasia was four months old, one of the nation's premier heart surgeons, who only lived forty-five minutes away, operated on her just before he relocated from the area. After the operation, she finally started to grow, but her heart was enlarging because it was working overtime, and the holes were enlarging as well. Leslie and her husband took Anastasia to Lourdes, France, when she was a year old. Six months later when they saw the heart specialist, the holes had closed, her heart was back to normal size, and she had grown in weight and height by 75 percent!

When I talked to Leslie shortly before Anastasia's second birthday, she told me that Anastasia had been the greatest gift to her family, particularly to her oldest son, as he learned to shift the focus from himself to his little sister. In fact, Leslie feels so privileged that she thinks others should be envious of her!

Has the script change been painful for Leslie? Yes. She's experienced a collage of disappointment, fear, hurt, and near death. But through life not going her way, God brought Leslie to a place of even deeper trust and hope in him. She drew closer to God. She shared her joys and sorrows with him, and that has taken her deeper into prayer and confident trust.

9/11 HERO. In the summer of 2003, I went to the graduation ceremony at Villanova University in Philadelphia. One of the graduation speakers was Suzanne Berger. For Suzanne and her husband, James, September 11, 2001, began as an ordinary day, just as it did for most of the rest of the world. However, her husband worked at 2 World Trade Center. She told us that after the first tower was hit, an announcement was made in Tower 2 for everyone to stay where they were and to continue working. (I know this is unimaginable now, but at the time, no one knew exactly what had happened, and they wanted to avoid a chaotic stampede.) However, something within her husband, James, told him disaster was on the horizon. He left his desk and began to herd people out of their offices. He refused to let them stay. He pulled them out from behind their desks; he made them get on the elevator and leave or go down the stairs.

But James himself didn't make it out alive. Suzanne said something very beautiful at the graduation that stuck in my mind. She said 9/11 showed the rest of the world what she and her three sons already knew—that James was a hero, that he was unselfish, that he put others first. And because he put others first, 156 of his fellow employees survived that day.[4]

Did the script change for Suzanne? You bet it did. Were there dreams that died that day on September 11? Absolutely. Did she turn her back on God? I'm sure there were moments of shock, disbelief, and unimaginable grief, but she was able to see God's hand even in the midst of the pain and suffering; she was able to see the gift of life that her husband gave to 156 other people and how God has sustained her through events she thought she'd never have to face. Pain and tragedy propelled her into a deeper relationship with God, into deeper prayer. She learned to surrender to the eyes of faith, to open the eye of her heart to see God even when God seemed absent to the rest of the world.

I hope these stories bring you hope and build up your faith, as they do for me. They also remind me that others have walked the journey before me and have survived. No, I take that back. They have thrived. They have allowed the pain and suffering of a changed script, combined with the healing power of time and grace, to discover that lemonade can be made of lemons.

And yet it's not easy when you're right in the midst of it. One day I received an e-mail message from a woman who told me that her seventeen-year-old son had been killed in a car crash by a drunken driver. It ripped a huge hole in her life that has remained a huge hole. Most days she feels that life isn't worth living, and she struggles with thoughts of suicide. Nothing seems to help the pain. And most of all, she doesn't understand why God let it happen. The script of life suddenly changed, not because of her own choice or her son's choice, but because of someone else's choice. Random evil ripped apart her life.

When evil, especially random evil, rips into our lives, it can feel like a hurricane trying to blow us away from God. The death, pain, and suffering that evil and injustice bring seem so senseless. We really don't see any reason to pray because it seems hopeless. How could God possibly answer my prayer?

CREATED FOR MEANING

I remember hearing a story about some prisoners in a concentration camp who were subjected to very hard manual labor.

Then one day, they were told to move a pile of dirt and rubble from site A to site B. The next day, they were told to move the same pile back to site A. The next day, they had to move it back to site B. And so it continued. They moved the pile back and forth from site A to site B and back to site A again for absolutely no purpose. Some of the men, who had endured much more difficult labor, went mad. Why? Because the work was meaningless. It was senseless, and this is what crushed and snuffed out their spirits.

God has created us as human persons in a very particular way—we were created for meaning. As long as something has meaning, we can endure any hardship, suffering, or sacrifice. Any woman who has given birth knows it's called "labor" for a very good reason! And yet, we endure the pain of childbirth for a purpose—to bring forth new life.

The American pilgrims and pioneers endured bitter hardship, including harsh winters, disease, and death, because they had a purpose—to build a new life, a better life, not just for themselves, but for their children and their children's children. James Berger and the other heroes of 9/11 suffered and sacrificed their lives, not for something trivial like better cell phones or lunch at McDonald's, but in order to protect life and freedom for others, for us. Their lives—and their deaths—had a meaning and purpose.

We're no different. We're created with this insatiable thirst for meaning and purpose. Each one of our souls says, "I thirst"—"I thirst to understand, to make meaning and sense out of the events and circumstances and injustices of life."

This is the beauty of prayer—it helps us to make sense out of the events and circumstances and injustices of life. In prayer, not only do we talk to God, but God talks to us. Not only do we share our thoughts and feelings with God, but he shares his thoughts and feelings with us. Not only do we draw closer to God, but God draws closer to us. One of the most precious ways this happens for Catholics is through Eucharistic adoration. Another marvelous way is through the word of God, the Bible.

Script Changes in Scripture

The Bible, especially the Old Testament, is one script change after another. Take Abraham, for instance. He was a wealthy merchant in Ur when God called him to go to an unknown land. At age seventy-five, God promised him an heir and said that his descendants would be "as numerous as the stars" (Genesis 26:4). But first, he and Sarah had to wait . . . and wait . . . and wait. They moved. They spent time in Egypt. They had no children, and still they had no children. They had to believe that *God was working . . . all the time*, even if they couldn't see it. They had to have hearts of hope even when all the evidence seemed to the contrary.

And God was faithful. He fulfilled his promise when Abraham was one hundred years old and Sarah's womb was as good as dead. Precisely through the script change, through what *wasn't* in the plan, God brought about the fulfillment of his plan and blessed the whole world through Abraham.

Then there's Noah. One day God showed up and asked him to build an ark, and his neighbors thought it was the craziest thing in the world. They were stuck in their categories of thinking: "Hey, Noah, I think you'd better hurry because I see a little cloud on the horizon" (snicker, snicker). However, they weren't snickering for long. When the flood came, God used the script change in Noah's life to preserve the entire human race.

Moses constantly had to adjust to life not going his way. He went from a basket in the Nile to being Pharaoh's son to wandering as a shepherd to meeting God in the burning bush to delivering the Israelites out of slavery. His life was one script change after another, one category change after another.

And what about David? I think the script he was writing went something like this: watch sheep, play my harp, find a beautiful woman to marry, have a bunch of kids, and stay out of the limelight. Instead he found himself king of Israel, and he led the whole Hebrew nation in psalms of prayer. He led them closer to God, and God blessed the Hebrew nation through him.

The prophets Jonah, Jeremiah, Hosea, and Isaiah all provide Oscar-winning script material. Jonah ran away from God and ended up in the belly of a whale. Jeremiah protested that he was too young to be a prophet. Hosea was asked by God to marry a prostitute. Isaiah thought he was doomed because he had seen the glory of the Lord. Over and over, the same scriptural pattern emerges: the invitation to wait and wait even while it appears as if nothing is happening. Then one day—boom!—circumstances come together and congeal, and God's plan is realized in a way far beyond our comprehension. It's kind of like making chocolate pudding: you stir and stir, and wait and wait, and it appears as if nothing is happening and then suddenly everything congeals, and it's delicious. So the next time you feel as if nothing is happening and God is tarrying, just remind yourself that you (and God) are making chocolate pudding, and no amount of fretting or anxious control will make the circumstances congeal any faster.

The entire Old Testament is simply preparation for the greatest script change of all time: the incarnation. Who would have dared to suggest that God would become man—that the invisible, unapproachable Holy One would take on human flesh? And, of course, this would have been impossible without Mary.

Talk about a script change! While Mary was betrothed to Joseph, the angel Gabriel invited her to conceive the Son of God by the power of the Holy Spirit. Instead of sharing the intimacies of birth with her mother and relatives, she shared them with Joseph, cows, and shepherds. The joy of consecrating her newborn son to God was interrupted by Simeon's prophecy of sorrow. As a new mother, she was forced to flee her homeland and raise her son in Egypt, a foreign land. And ultimately, Mary stood at the foot of the cross, not turning away from God, not clinging to her own categories, but turning toward God, pressing into God, deepening her dialogue with God by offering the body and blood of her Son on the cross back to the Father.

Changing the Way We Pray

When I recognized that this was the pattern of Scripture, that it was one script change after another, I realized I needed to change the way I pray. Most of my life, my prayer has focused on protecting the script I was writing. "Dear God, this is what *I* want. Now please bless it." Or "Dear God, this is what *I* think should happen. Now please make it happen." Instead, I realized what I really need to pray is "O God, please change the script," because that's how God's plan can be realized, that's how he can change the course of history, and that's how I can turn toward him and be led into even deeper prayer and dialogue with him.

And there has been no scarcity of script changes in my life. My life *definitely* didn't go the way I wanted. I was born and raised in San Diego, California, in a wonderful Catholic family. At age sixteen, I had the great privilege of encountering God in a personal way through a weekend retreat experience. At eighteen, I graduated as valedictorian of my high school class of five hundred; at nineteen, I married my high school sweetheart; and at twenty-one, my husband and I moved to Steubenville, Ohio, so that I could study theology at the Franciscan University of Steubenville. Five years later, after I had finished my degree, our wonderful son Michael was born. The script of life was going just as planned (two thumbs up!). I had a good husband, a wonderful son, Christian fellowship, intellectual stimulation, supportive relationships, and a home in a nice neighborhood.

Then the script changed (two thumbs down). For many years, my husband had struggled with his personal identity. God had intervened at certain crisis points, and the issue would go underground for a while, but then it would pop up again. I had run out of strategies: we had moved, we had joined a Catholic community of families, we had started our family, but still the issue kept resurfacing.

When my son Michael was almost three, we agreed on a temporary separation with the intention of getting back together. Over the next year, I went through one of the darkest periods in my life. My mind was so saturated with pain that I couldn't even think of praying in a conversational way. Perhaps you've been through a similar dark period, or you're going through one right now—in which God seems hidden behind a veil of impenetrable clouds, or you feel as if you're sinking into the pit of despair, and you're not Indiana Jones, who can craftily figure his way out. Instead, life seems dark, hopeless, and confused.

That's the way I felt. With my marriage failing, I felt as if someone had taken my identity, placed it on a table, and smashed it into a million pieces. How could I ever regain my sense of wholeness and zest for life? How could my future be anything but a painful last-place finish?

Answer: I had to change my categories of thinking. On my

birthday that year, God rearranged the furniture of my mind when he showed me that I was first a daughter, then a bride. *First* a daughter, *then* a bride—what a radical shift in my identity! Somewhere along my feminine path I'd forgotten the most fundamental truth of my life—that before being a wife, mother, cook, chauffeur, or teacher, I was first a daughter of the Father. God in his mercy ripped out the faulty foundation of straw and hay that he knew couldn't endure the storms of life and replaced it with an indestructible one of gold and precious stones.

Like a skillful potter, God remolded my identity into the grace-filled shape he had intended from all eternity. Best of all, he gave me a new life that wasn't based on getting my prayers answered or on having life go the way I thought it should, but on my relationship with him. This unwelcome script change has become *the* defining moment of my adult life. Most important, what *wasn't* in my script has provided the stabilizing bolts for the roller coaster of script changes that has followed.

In life-splintering moments like these, we can be like the Pharisees and close our minds and hearts to God, or we can change our categories of thinking. We can open our minds and hearts to a new way of thinking. Here's the image I like to use—that of a magnifying glass. If we look at our circumstances through a magnifying glass, then our circumstances become the biggest thing in our lives. We can't see anything else. But if we turn the magnifying glass away from our circumstances to God and make him the biggest thing in our lives, then we can see the goodness of God, and we can have hope, no matter how dire or desperate the circumstances.

Questions for Reflection and Discussion:

1. What thoughts or ideas struck you in this chapter?

2. What's your reaction to this statement: "The primary purpose of prayer is not to get our prayers answered but to grow in a deeper relationship with God"?

3. How has the script of your life changed?

4. Have your script changes brought you deeper into a relationship with God or drawn you away from him?

5. Can you think of other biblical script changes?

6. Take a moment, and pray for God to change your categories of thinking so that he becomes the biggest reality in your life.

CHAPTER 3

THE WAY OF THE CROSS

One day I was browsing through an antique store in a small midwestern town when my eye caught sight of a pair of old wire-rimmed glasses that had only one lens. When I placed it on the counter to purchase it, the cashier tried to convince me to buy a similar pair that had both lenses intact. I smiled and politely refused her offer. I wanted to use the glasses when I give retreats and conferences to make a point: in order to navigate the script changes of life, we have to look through the lenses of both hope *and* patience. If we only have a heart of hope *or* a heart of patience, then it's like trying to look through just one lens. The world is skewed, and we get a headache!

But what does a heart of hope and patience look like? Fortunately we don't have to search too far to find it, because it's on the cross. Jesus, on the cross, had every reason to doubt God's goodness, to be angry and bitter at the script change of life. And we might even think that Jesus gave in to these thoughts, since Matthew 27:46 says that Jesus cried out on the cross, "Eli, Eli, lema sabachthani?" "My God, my God, why have you abandoned me?"

It almost sounds as if Jesus is despairing of God's presence, but I don't think he is. He's actually quoting the first line of Psalm 22. "My God, my God, why have you abandoned me?" is not the end of the psalm, but just the beginning. It would be like me saying, "Oh, say can you see . . ." You wouldn't say, "Oh, say can you see what, Katrina?" You would know that I'm quoting the first line of the United States national anthem, "The Star-Spangled Banner." You would know there's more to come. The same is true of Jesus. There are more than thirty additional verses in that psalm. And this is not a psalm of despair but of hope. In fact, it's an incredible dialogue between suffering and hope.

Let's look at the rest of this psalm. After this initial cry of abandonment, the psalmist proclaims, beginning in verse four:

> Yet you are enthroned as the Holy One;
>   you are the glory of Israel.
> In you our ancestors trusted;
>   they trusted and you rescued them.
> To you they cried out and they escaped;
>   in you they trusted and were not disappointed. (22:4-6)

He's professing the goodness of God. But then in verse seven, the rhythm changes back to describing his sufferings:

> But I am a worm, hardly human,
>   scorned by everyone, despised by the people.
> All who see me mock me;
>   they curl their lips and jeer;
>   they shake their heads at me:

"You relied on the LORD—let him deliver you;
    if he loves you, let him rescue you." (22:7-9)

The mockers are saying: "God isn't good. God doesn't love you. If he did, you wouldn't be enduring this." But the psalmist refuses to be drawn into their taunts. Instead he says to God:

Yet you drew me forth from the womb,
    made me safe at my mother's breast.
Upon you I was thrust from the womb;
    since birth you are my God. (22:10-11)

The description of suffering continues in verse fifteen:

Like water my life drains away;
    all my bones grow soft.
My heart has become like wax,
    it melts away within me. (22:15)

And again in verses seventeen and eighteen:

Many dogs surround me;
    a pack of evildoers closes in on me.
So wasted are my hands and feet
    that I can count all my bones. (22:17-18)

Now, after this third description of suffering and evil, does the psalmist curse God? No; he says in verse twenty-three: "Then I will proclaim your name to the assembly; / in the community I will praise you." Verse twenty-six continues: "I will offer praise in the great assembly; / my vows I will fulfill before those who fear him." And he finishes in verse thirty-two by proclaiming: "The generation to come will be told of the Lord, / that they may proclaim to a people yet unborn / the deliverance you have brought."

This is a psalm of hope. Jesus wasn't disconnected from the Father; he was clinging to the Father. However, the hard thing about having a heart of hope is that it must be joined to a heart of patience, to the other lens. Romans 8:24-25 says: "Now hope that sees for itself is not hope. For who hopes for what one sees? But if we hope for what we do not see, we wait with [patient] endurance."

GOD IS WORKING

Hope means we believe that "God is working . . . all the time," even when we can't see it. The temptation with suffering and pain is to allow it to crush us and convince us that God doesn't care about us, that he's somewhere far removed from our pain and suffering. He's the clock maker who wound up the earth and set it going on its own, and just sits up in heaven watching all of us fumble around.

However, suffering should do just the opposite. Instead of being disconnected from God, we should cling to God. Suffering should remind us that God is working (all the time), even when we can't see it. Instead of walking a-way from the cross, we should walk the way of the cross.

Romans 8:28 captures the idea of God being at work all the time. It says, "We know that all things work for good for those who love God, who are called according to his purpose." God is working, working, working (all the time): arranging things over here, offering grace over there, inviting us to change our categories of thinking, trying to open our hearts and minds to the bigger picture, trying to get us to turn the magnifying glass away from our circumstances and toward him. When we look at the cross, our hearts should swell with a hope that says, "God is working all the time"—even when it's not immediately obvious, even when we have to wait (and wait) for God's plan to be fulfilled.

Put yourself in the shoes of the disciples on Good Friday. Your master, lord, and messiah has just been brutally beaten, tortured, and crucified. He's dead, buried, and gone. God the Father could have raised Jesus immediately from the dead; he could have given Abraham a child right away; he could have sent rain for Noah right away, but he didn't. Abraham, Noah, and the disciples had to wait.

And the disciples were discouraged. They'd forgotten the most important truth: that God is working . . . all the time. In fact, two of them were walking *away* from Jerusalem to Emmaus (Luke 24), walking away from God's promises, because they were so lacking in hope. Jesus appears to them and joins them on the road. Notice he doesn't criticize them and say, "You're so stupid. Why don't you just have more hope?" Instead, he opens their minds to Scripture; he interprets for them every passage of Scripture that refers to him. He turns the magnifying glass to God.

As this is happening, the two disciples are beginning to sense a change within themselves, a stirring of hope. When they sit down to eat and Jesus breaks the bread, Scripture says, "With that their eyes were opened and they recognized him" (Luke 24:31). Their eyes were opened, and they exclaimed to each other, "Were not our hearts burning (within us) while he spoke to us on the way and opened the scriptures to us?" (24:32).

Their hearts were burning. That's a heart filled with hope. A heart that burns with the conviction that God is working . . . all the time, to make everything work together for the good, even if we can't see it at that present moment. A heart of hope is a heart that presses into God and stays connected instead of drawing away.

God wants to give you the same heart, a heart burning with the conviction that God is working all the time, that he exists and that he can redeem *anything*—hurricanes, adultery, addiction, birth defects, AIDS, children leaving the Church, hot flashes— even when you can't see it, even when you have to be patient, even when you have to wait upon God for the meaning and purpose to be revealed.

WAITING WITH PURPOSE

Fr. Henri Nouwen has a minijewel of a book entitled *The Path of Waiting*. I could never have written this booklet; I am an impatient person. Fr. Nouwen must have secretly followed me around and then captured what he saw when he says that impatient people are always expecting the real thing to happen "somewhere else and therefore want to go elsewhere. The moment is empty."[1]

Perhaps you were born with a patient odometer, content to be in the present moment and not ticking off the miles, but I wasn't. This is another reason why God graciously allows script changes in my life—to drag me out of *my* future plans and into the present moment. God keeps inviting me to leave behind the kingdoms I am building in my mind and to be actively available to the world around me. Fr. Nouwen says, "Active waiting means to be present fully to the moment, in the conviction that something is happening where you are and that you want to be present to it. A waiting person is someone who is present to the moment, who believes that this moment is *the moment*."[2]

Why is this so agonizing? Because, as Fr. Nouwen says, this type of waiting is open ended. It is the "willingness to stay where we are and live the situation out to the full in the belief that something hidden there will manifest itself to us."[3] In contrast, most of our waiting is not open ended, but a way of controlling the future, of doing the things that will make our desired outcome, our wishes, take place. We have to "let go of [our] wishes," Fr. Nouwen says, "and start hoping."[4]

Ouch! Frankly, I don't want to let go of my wishes because then I feel as if I'm falling into a black hole without purpose or direction. But that's where I'm wrong. Waiting is not meant to be an unmoored state in which the winds of change smack us around and batter our humanity into smithereens. Waiting is meant to be anchored in hope, in the hope of *God's promises, not our wishes*. "People who wait have received a promise that allows them to wait," Fr. Nouwen reminds us. "They have received something that is at work in them, like a seed that has started to grow."[5]

What if you haven't received a promise that allows you to wait? In truth, you have. The Bible is full of promises that allow you to wait, promises of the goodness of God, promises of God working, even when you can't see it. If you are in a waiting period, grab your Bible and start reminding yourself of God's promises. Among these are God's promises to love us, to forgive us, to save us, to set us free from sin, to give us eternal life, to take care of our material needs, to guide us, to give us strength, to answer our prayers, and to protect us from the evil one.[6]

(GOD THE) FATHER KNOWS BEST

In addition, God can also deliver a personalized promise. For more than twenty years, I endured the cold winters in Ohio while the Southern Californian in me hibernated. Finally, when my son enrolled in college in our hometown, I was sprung from my winter cage. I re-nested in the Valley of the Sun (Phoenix, Arizona), where I enjoyed an unbroken string of 128 days without a cloud. Oh yes, God was definitely good . . . all the sunny time.

Four months later, my son visited me for Christmas. In the car on the way home from the airport, he broke the news: after one semester at a wonderful Catholic college, he'd been dismissed because of poor grades. In an instant, I felt smacked and battered. My college dreams for him splintered apart like thin ice, and I fell into the subzero water below, gasping for control of my life and his. Where would his life go from here? How could I fix the situation?

Everything within me ached to ditch my life in Arizona and head back to Ohio to rescue him, to put the pieces back together the way I thought they should be. Instead, I held onto my anchor of hope and prayed. I asked the Lord to give me a word, an insight, about my son. He told me, "I have him in the palm of my hand." What a divine reassurance! Then I asked for a word for me, and God the Father graciously reminded me: "I have big shoulders to cry on." My maternal heart suddenly had a promise and a place to take my pain.

I stood on that promise, believing that God had Michael in the palm of his hand, and I used those big shoulders (and lots of tissues) frequently. It gave me the strength to wait actively in the present moment, and to be open to new possibilities other than the "safe" Catholic education I had always wished for my only son.

The story does have a happy ending: God used the script change to redirect Michael to be a hair stylist and color special-ist, which he is enthusiastically pursuing. Moreover, since this is his father's field, Michael's masculine need for mentoring from his father is being fulfilled tenfold. In my wildest imagination, I never would have written the script this way. Thank goodness God didn't give in to my maternal tantrums! Thank goodness life doesn't always go my way.

OPEN TO ALL POSSIBILITIES

"The spiritual life," Fr. Nouwen says, "is a life in which we wait, actively present to the moment, expecting that new things will happen to us, new things that are far beyond our own imagination and prediction."[7] Isn't this the distilled descrip-tion of the Christian life? When we live in patience and hope, letting go of control, then our waiting can be open to *all* pos-sibilities. *God* can conceive new possibilities through you. He can change the course of history through you. He can help you let go of control so that you can allow him to run the universe (and your children's lives). He can even help you find joy in your crosses.

Hebrews 12:1-2 says: "Let us . . . persevere in running the race that lies before us while keeping our eyes fixed on Jesus, the leader and perfecter of faith. For the sake of the joy that lay before him he endured the cross, despising its shame, and has taken his seat at the right of the throne of God." The joy of the cross is the joy of knowing that suffering has a meaning and a purpose. You are not just moving a pile of rocks from Point A to Point B and back to Point A again. *You are not a victim.* God's plan for your life and your family isn't being ripped up like a piece of paper and thrown in the garbage. The way of the cross ends in victory, not in defeat. Good Friday is not the end of the story. Easter is coming!

Suffering is preparing you for what God has in store for you down the road. Suffering is forming in you a heart of hope and patience. Suffering is inviting you to turn the magnifying glass to God and make him the biggest thing in your life. Suffering is prying you away from white-knuckle control and leading you into the hands of God.

To illustrate how hard it can be to embrace this heart of hope and patience, I'd like to share a story by an obstetrician told in the first person:

This fragile young woman was in labor, and the baby was breech, coming out both feet first. The death rate for breech babies is comparatively high, so everyone in the room was tense. I gently drew down one little foot. I reached for the other, and to my consternation, I saw that the entire thigh from the hip to the knee was missing, and this leg reached down only to the opposite knee.

Then followed the hardest struggle I ever had with myself. I knew what a dreadful effect this would have on the nervous system of this unstable mother. Most of all, I saw this little girl sitting sadly by herself while other girls laughed and danced, ran and played, and I suddenly realized there was something that would save all this trouble, and it was in my power.

One breech baby in ten dies in delivery because it is not delivered rapidly enough. If I could make myself delay only a few short moments, she would be brain-dead. No one would ever know. The mother, after the first shock of grief, would probably be glad she lost a child so badly handicapped. She could try again. . . .

I motioned to the nurse for a towel to conceal from the attending nurses what my eyes alone had seen. With the touch of that pitiful little foot in my hand, a pang of sorrow for the baby's future swept through me, and my decision was made.

I glanced at the clock. Three of the eight minutes had already gone by. . . . Every eye was upon me and I could feel the tension in their eagerness to do instantly whatever I asked. Two or three more minutes would be enough. I drew the baby down a little lower to deliver the arms and, as I did so, the little pink foot on the good side bobbed out from the protecting towel and pressed firmly against my hand.

There was a sudden convulsive movement of the baby's body, a feeling of strength of life and vigor. It was too much. I couldn't do it. I delivered the baby with her pitiful little leg.

All my forebodings came true. The mother had a nervous breakdown. . . . They had gone to Rochester, Minnesota, to seek help for the girl. They had been to Chicago and Boston. Finally I lost track of them altogether.

As the years went on, I blamed myself bitterly for not having had the strength to yield to my temptation. But that was then, and today our hospital was staging an elaborate Christmas party. In came the nurses in their uniforms and caps. . . . Each held high a lighted candle, while through the auditorium floated the familiar strains of "Silent Night."

[On the stage,] there sat lovely musicians, all in shimmering white evening gowns. They played very softly an organ, a harp, a cello, and a violin. I am sure I was not the only old sissy there whose eyes were wet. I was especially fascinated by the young harpist. She played extraordinarily well, as if she loved it. Her slender fingers flicked across the strings. Her face was made beautiful by a mass of auburn hair; it was upturned as if the world at that moment were a wonderful and holy place.

When the program was over, I sat alone thinking, when running down the aisle came a woman I didn't know. She came to me with arms outstretched. "Oh, you saw her, you must have recognized your baby. That was my daughter who played the harp; I saw you watching her. Don't you remember the little girl who was born with only one good leg seventeen years ago? We tried everything at first, but now she has an entire artificial leg on that side—but you would never know it. She can walk, swim, and can almost dance. But, best of all, through all these years when she couldn't do those things other girls did, she learned to use her hands so wonderfully. She's going to be a great harpist. She's my whole life, and now she's so happy . . . and here she is!"

The sweet young girl had quietly approached, her eyes glowing. She stood beside me. "This is your first doctor, dear." The mother's voice trembled. I could see her literally swept back, as I was, through all the years of heartache to that day when I first showed her daughter to her.

Impulsively, I took the child in my arms. Across her warm young shoulders I saw the creeping hands of the clock in the delivery room seventeen years ago. I lived again those awful few minutes when her life was in my hands, when I had decided on deliberate infanticide, and then changed my mind. I held her away from me and looked at her. "You'll never know, my dear—you'll never know, nor will anyone else in all the world know, just what tonight means to me."[8]

This obstetrician initially focused only on what he could perceive as reality—the anticipated pain and suffering of a deformed child and her mother. As the course of events unfolded, things got worse before they got better. How often this is the case for us humans, who experience and perceive life in the confines of time! We only experience a segment, a thin slice of reality at a time. God, however, is working across the boundary of time in ways that we can't imagine and sometimes may never know. A heart of hope must be joined to a heart of patience, one that is willing to wait for God's plan to be fulfilled.

As you finish this chapter, I invite you to do three things:

1. Make peace with God over the script changes that have already occurred in your life. If you are Catholic, go to the Sacrament of Reconciliation and bring to God all the hurt, bitterness, anger, disappointment, and unforgiveness that have prevented you from accepting life not going your way. If you are not Catholic, you can write a letter to God expressing the same sentiments and then burn it (or flush it down the toilet!) as a way of letting go. Grieve what needs to be grieved, and then breathe the clean, possibility-laden air of God's promises.

2. Bring to the cross all your doubts and even your despair. Ask God to change your categories of thinking. Ask him for a heart of hope, a heart that burns with the conviction that God is working (all the time), even when you can't see it. Ask for a heart that's patient, that's willing to wait for God's plan to be fulfilled.

3. After Cardinal John O'Connor was ordained bishop of New York City, Mother Teresa exhorted him, "Give God permission."[9] I invite you to do the same thing: give God permission. Give him permission to change the script of your life. Ask for the grace to pray, "God, please change the script," because then, no matter what life hands you, you'll find a new surrender and a joyful freedom that comes from pressing into the heart of God. You'll be filled with an anticipation that comes from God's plan being fulfilled and not your own, especially when life doesn't go the way you expected.

Questions for Reflection and Discussion:

1. What is your reaction to the story of the obstetrician?

2. Why is it so hard to have a heart of hope and patience?

3. Can you give an example in your own life or someone else's life where God was working (all the time), even when it wasn't evident?

4. Do you consider yourself a patient person? Why or why not? How can you grow in patience?

5. What would be the worst "cross" you could imagine having to bear? Which of God's promises could help you make it through this suffering?

6. Take time to read the following psalm, and then pour your heart out before God in prayer.

> Only in God be at rest, my soul
>   for from him comes my hope.
> He only is my rock and my salvation,
>   my stronghold; I shall not be disturbed.
> With God is my safety and my glory,
>   he is the rock of my strength; My refuge is in God.
> Trust in him at all times, O my people!
>   Pour out your hearts before him; God is our refuge!
> (Psalm 62:6-9)[10]

CHAPTER 4

THE EUCHARISTIC PATTERN

In order to embrace life when it's not going the way we want, we need not only a heart of hope and patience that believes God is working (all the time) but the rock-solid conviction that God is with us . . . all the time.

This conviction animated Jesus' life, especially in the Gospel of John, where Jesus constantly talks about his relationship with the Father. In John 16:32, Jesus says, "But I am not alone, because the Father is with me." In the parable of the prodigal son, we see a similar refrain. The father goes out to the elder son, who refuses to come to the younger son's celebration, and the father's first words to the elder son are: "My son, you are here with me always" (Luke 15:31). Jesus, before his ascension into heaven, tells his disciples, "And behold, I am with you always, until the end of the age" (Matthew 28:20). We must be animated by the same conviction: we can never be alone; God is with us all the time.

How is this possible? How is it possible for God to be with us all the time?

GOD SEARCHES FOR US

There's a remarkable truth about Christianity that sets it apart from all other religions. In other religions, man goes searching for

God, but in Christianity, God comes searching for man. This is the incredible truth of the incarnation—that God became man and dwelt among us. Or as John 1:14 says, "And we saw his glory, the glory as of the Father's only Son, full of grace and truth."

However, that's not the end of the story. Jesus didn't just come and live among us so that he could quietly spend his time in Nazareth as a master carpenter. He had a different mission, and that mission was to save us, to offer his body and blood on the cross for the forgiveness of our sins. Jesus gave up his life for us to bring us back into the family of God. But that's not the end of the story either.

Throughout the Gospel of John, Jesus promises to send another Comforter, who will lead the disciples into all truth. At the moment of Jesus' death, John chooses his words with heart-surgeon precision: "When Jesus had taken the wine, he said, 'It is finished.' And bowing his head, he handed over the spirit" (John 19:30).

Then, when Jesus appeared to the disciples after his resurrection, John says Jesus breathed on them and said, "Receive the holy Spirit" (John 20:22). Jesus' death on the cross breathes the Spirit of God back into us! Whereas we forfeited sanctifying grace (God's Spirit within us) through original sin, John bends over backwards to tell us that God's Spirit is breathed into our spirit again.

But that's not the end of the story either.

In the Jewish Seder meal, there's a beautiful prayer called "Dayyenu." *Dayyenu* is Hebrew for "It would have been enough for us." During the Seder meal, the host recounts a wonder of God, and the rest of the family responds, "Dayyenu—it would have been enough." It's a beautiful litany with a verse and response that goes like this:

Had he brought us out from Egypt, and not executed judgment against the Egyptians,

It would have been enough.

Had he executed judgment against the Egyptians and not divided the sea for us,

It would have been enough.

Had he divided the sea for us and not drowned our oppressors in it,

It would have been enough.

Had he drowned our oppressors in it, and not helped us forty years in the desert,

It would have been enough.

Had he fed us manna, and not brought us to Mount Sinai,

It would have been enough.

Had he brought us to Mount Sinai, and not given us the Law,

It would have been enough.

Had he given us the Law, and not brought us into the Promised Land,

It would have been enough.

Had he brought us into the Promised Land, and not given us the Temple,

It would have been enough.

As believers in Jesus Christ, we can continue this marvelous litany with our own Christian additions:

Had he given us the Temple and not sent us his Son, the Messiah,

It would have been enough.

Had he sent us his Son, and not given him up to die for our sins on the cross,

It would have been enough.

Had he given up his Son to die for our sins on the cross, and not raised him from the dead,

It would have been enough.

Had he raised him from the dead and not sent his Holy Spirit,

It would have been enough.

Would that have been enough? Yes! Yes! But there's one thing more:

Had he sent his Holy Spirit, and not left his Real Presence among us in the Eucharist,

It would have been enough.

GOD REMAINS AMONG US

God didn't have to remain among us in the Eucharist. It would have been enough to send his Spirit and remain among us spiritually. But that wasn't enough for God. He wanted to be as close to us as *humanly* possible. As human persons, we are not just spirit. That would make us angels. We are body and spirit, and so God desired to remain among us according to our nature, both body and spirit.

That's why at the Last Supper, Jesus said, "This is my body, which will be given for you" (Luke 22:19). Jesus makes a *bodily* gift of self to us that is permanent and irrevocable. It's not temporary or intermittent like Morse code—now he's here, now he's not, now he's here, now he's not. His gift of self, of his body and blood, is permanent and irrevocable.

That is why Catholics believe the Eucharist isn't just bread and wine. It really is the body and blood of Christ under the appearance of bread and wine. Jesus is true to his word: "Behold, I am with you always, until the end of the age" (Matthew 28:20). God is with us (all the time), both body and spirit in the Eucharist, until the end of the world.

Throughout his pontificate, Pope John Paul II invited the universal Church to rediscover the Eucharist as the source and summit of the Christian life. In his 2003 encyclical on the Eucharist, *Ecclesia de Eucharistica*, Pope John Paul II wrote: "Proclaiming the death of the Lord 'until he comes' (1 Corinthians 11:26) entails that all who take part in the Eucharist be committed to changing their lives and making them in a certain way completely 'Eucharistic.'"[1]

The Eucharistic Pattern

How can we do this? How can we make our lives completely Eucharistic? How can we anchor our very being in the Eucharistic mystery? The answer is to allow the Eucharistic mystery to be inscribed into our very lives.

What do I mean? In Philippians 3:10, St. Paul says: "I wish to know Christ and the power flowing from his resurrection; likewise to know how to share in his sufferings by being formed into the pattern of his death."[2] Notice that there's a very particular rhythm here: before we can know the power flowing from Christ's resurrection, we have to first share in the pattern of his death. A bit later in Philippians, St. Paul says, "He [Jesus Christ] will change our lowly body to conform with his glorified body" (3:21). Christ wants to remake the pattern of our mortal bodies into the pattern of his glorified body, and this is the Eucharistic pattern.

There's another wonderful book by Fr. Henri Nouwen entitled *Life of the Beloved*. I'd like to use this book as a powerful spotlight to illuminate the Eucharistic pattern. Here's how Fr. Nouwen begins:

To identify the movements of the Spirit in our lives, I have found it helpful to use four words: taken [chosen], blessed, broken, and given. . . . These words also summarize my life as a Christian because, as a Christian, I am called to become bread for the world: bread that is taken, blessed, broken and given. Most importantly, however, they summarize my life as a human being because in every moment of my life somewhere, somehow the taking, the blessing, the breaking and the giving are happening.[3]

That's the Eucharistic pattern. That's how Christ wants to remake the pattern of our bodies according to the pattern of his crucified and glorified body—by being chosen, blessed, broken, and given.

Chosen!

First, being chosen. What does it mean to be chosen? Think of Miss America: "There she is, Miss America!" She is no longer just one of the crowd; she is chosen, selected from the crowd. God wants to do the same thing for us. In God's eyes, we are each Miss America. You are not just one of the crowd of six billion people on this earth; you are selected from the crowd.

When Jesus was baptized in the Jordan, the heavens opened, and a voice proclaimed, "You are my beloved Son" (Luke 3:22). At your baptism, the heavens opened and a voice proclaimed (even if you couldn't hear it), "This is my beloved daughter." This is my beloved! You are chosen by God the Father. Because of the Father's great love, you are selected from among the crowd. Here's how Fr. Nouwen says it: "When I know that I am chosen, I know that I have been seen as a special person. Someone has noticed me in my uniqueness and has expressed a desire to know me, to come closer to me, to love me."[4]

That is what the Father is saying to you. He has noticed you in your uniqueness; he has expressed a desire to know you, to come closer to you, to love you. He has chosen *you*. That's why he sent his Son to die and rise again, and that's why he sent his Spirit—so you could be his beloved.

This can be so hard for us to hear because we think we have to "do" something to be the beloved—we have to be the most talented, the prettiest, the friendliest, the holiest, the most gifted at prayer. But we don't because you can't earn belovedness. You can't win it, and you can't lose it. It's a gift. God's *gift* from all eternity is choosing you as his beloved.

A wonderful Protestant speaker, Marilyn Meburg, is fond of saying, "Jesus didn't notice performance; he noticed persons." Jesus doesn't notice our performance, he notices our belovedness. The classical example of this in the New Testament is the woman caught in adultery (John 8). If Jesus had noticed performance, he would have said to the men who dragged the woman before him, "Yeah, you're right. She's guilty. Stone her!" But he didn't notice performance, he noticed the person, and so he said, "Let the one among you who is without sin be the first to throw a stone at her." Then, after all her accusers left, he turned to the woman and said, "Woman, where are they? Has no one condemned you?" "No one, sir," she replied. Then Jesus said, "Neither do I condemn you. Go, [and] from now on do not sin any more" (see 8:3-11). Instead of condemnation and shame, this woman experienced being chosen by Christ. She experienced her dignity being restored as the beloved.

We see a similar scenario in the New Testament with someone very short—Zacchaeus (see Luke 19). If Jesus were noticing performance, he probably would have walked right by Zacchaeus and ignored this greedy, dishonest tax collector. But he didn't. Instead, he noticed his belovedness, and so he said to Zacchaeus, "Come down quickly, for today I must stay at your house" (19:5). Can you imagine Zacchaeus' joy at being chosen? At being selected from the crowd?

In the parable of the prodigal son (Luke 15), Jesus shows us how the father wasn't interested in performance. When his wayward son came home, he didn't grill him by asking, "What did you do with my money? How much do you have left? Do you have anything to show for it?" Instead, he ran out to meet him and threw his arms around him. He called for a robe, sandals, and the family ring. He welcomed him back into the family, not because of his performance, but because of his person.

And this is what angered the elder son so much. The elder son said (in my paraphrase), "What do you mean, you're going to welcome him back into the family after he wasted all your money? And what about me? Look at all I've done to earn and deserve your love! What about my performance?" This son was totally caught up in performance. But the father wasn't. The father in the parable is, of course, an image of God the Father, who notices our belovedness before our performance.

And then there's Martha and Mary in Luke 10. Martha comes to Jesus as the perfect domestic martyr and says, "Jesus, notice my performance. I'm cooking! I'm cleaning! I'm working hard! And Mary is just sitting there doing nothing!" And Jesus says to her, "Martha, Martha, I appreciate your hard work, but what I really love is you. It's your *person* that's important to me, not your performance."

Each of these people (the woman caught in adultery, Zacchaeus, the prodigal son, Martha) experienced themselves as being loved and chosen, not because of any merit or performance of their own, but through the pure gift of God in Jesus Christ. A striking line I heard once in a homily in Canada encapsulates this truth: "The beloved has nothing to prove." As the beloved, you have nothing to prove to God of your worthiness. He loves your person.

Blessed!

We're not only chosen, but we're also blessed. Fr. Nouwen says, "It is not enough to be chosen. We also need an ongoing blessing that allows us to hear in an ever-new way that we belong to a loving God who will never leave us alone."[5]

I remember hearing a story once about a couple who had been married for forty-four years. One day the husband overheard his wife on the phone, telling a friend with a sigh, "He hasn't told me he loves me in forty-four years." After she hung up the phone, the husband gave his defense: "I told you on our wedding day that I loved you and that if I ever changed my mind, I'd let you know."

But that's not sufficient, to be told once that we're loved, is it? The Eucharistic bread is not only chosen but blessed. So, too, God designed us not only to be chosen, but blessed—to hear ongoing words of blessing, ongoing affirmation that we are valued and loved.

In our culture, many of us are famished for blessing. We're starving to have our intrinsic value—not our utilitarian value—affirmed. Unfortunately, most Americans usually acquire their social value through external measurements, such as work accomplishments, the number of zeros in their salary, a beautiful four-thousand-square-foot home, or bright, successful children.

But God's design is different. God's desire for us is to hear words of blessing for who we are and to experience being blessed. In fact, Scripture says the first thing God did after he created male and female was to bless them (see Genesis 1:28). He affirmed their intrinsic value, their being made in his image and likeness. He affirmed their belonging to himself.

We even see this pattern in Jesus' life. Not only was he blessed at his baptism, but God the Father declared Jesus' belovedness a second time at the transfiguration (see Matthew 17). Again the heavens opened, and God proclaimed, "This is my beloved Son" (17:5). Jesus is not only the Messiah, the "Chosen One," but also the "Blessed One." He experienced ongoing affirmation from the Father. I suspect that Jesus withdrew into the desert for long nights of prayer precisely for this reason—to experience the Father's blessing and affirmation.

The same is true for us. We need to experience ongoing words of blessing that remind us that we are highly valued. We need to give and receive not only compliments (which value something we've done or a skill we have), but also, and most especially, *affirmation*, which values our "be-ing," who we are *apart* from anything we do.

The following true story about the hidden effect of affirmation was told by a junior high math teacher, Sr. Helen Mrosla:

One Friday, things just didn't feel right. We had worked hard on a new concept all week, and I sensed that the students were frowning, frustrated with themselves and edgy with one another. I had to stop this crankiness before it got out of hand. So I asked them to list the names of the other students in the room on two sheets of paper, leaving a space between each name. Then I told them to think of the nicest thing they could say about each of their classmates and write it down. It took the remainder of the class period to finish their assignment, and as the students left the room, each one handed me the papers. Charlie smiled. Mark said, "Thank you for teaching me, Sister. Have a good weekend." That Saturday, I wrote down the name of each student on a separate sheet of paper, and I listed what everyone else had said about that individual.

On Monday I gave each student his or her list. Before long, the entire class was smiling. "Really?" I heard whispered. "I never knew that meant anything to anyone!" "I didn't know others liked me so much." No one ever mentioned those papers in class again. I never knew if they discussed them after class or with their parents, but it didn't matter. The exercise had accomplished its purpose. The students were happy with themselves and one another again.

That group of students moved on. Several years later, after I returned from vacation, my parents met me at the airport. As we were driving home, Mother asked me the usual questions about the trip, the weather, my experiences in general. There was a lull in the conversation. Mother gave Dad a sideways glance and simply said, "Dad?" My father cleared his throat as he usually did before something important. "The Eklunds called last night," he began. "Really?" I said. "I haven't heard from them in years. I wonder how Mark is." Dad responded quietly. "Mark was killed in Vietnam," he said. "The funeral is tomorrow, and his parents would like it if you could attend." To this day I can still point to the exact spot on I-494 where Dad told me about Mark.

I had never seen a serviceman in a military coffin before. Mark looked so handsome, so mature. . . . The church was packed with Mark's friends. Chuck's sister sang "The Battle Hymn of the Republic." Why did it have to rain on the day of the funeral? It was difficult enough at the graveside. The pastor said the usual prayers, and the bugler played taps. One by one those who loved Mark took a last walk by the coffin and sprinkled it with holy water. I was the last one to bless the coffin. As I stood there, one of the soldiers who acted as pallbearer came up to me. "Were you Mark's math teacher?" he asked. I nodded as I continued to stare at the coffin. "Mark talked about you a lot," he said.

After the funeral, most of Mark's former classmates headed to Chuck's farmhouse for lunch. Mark's mother and father were there, obviously waiting for me. "We want to show you something," his father said, taking a wallet out of his pocket. "They found this on Mark when he was killed. We thought you might recognize it." Opening the billfold, he carefully removed two worn pieces of notebook paper that had obviously been taped, folded, and refolded many times. I knew without looking that the papers were the ones on which I had listed all the good things each of Mark's classmates had said about him. "Thank you so much for doing that," Mark's mother said. "As you can see, Mark treasured it."

Mark's classmates started to gather around us. Charlie smiled rather sheepishly and said, "I still have my list. I keep it in the top drawer of my desk at home." Chuck's wife said, "Chuck asked me to put his in our wedding album." "I have mine too," Marilyn said. "It's in my diary." Then Vicki, another classmate, reached into her pocketbook, took out her wallet and showed her worn and frazzled list to the group. "I carry this with me at all times," Vicki said without batting an eyelash. "I think we all saved our lists."[6]

These classmates experienced the value of being blessed, of being affirmed in their intrinsic worth. And it was something they literally carried with them the rest of their lives.

When I realized the importance of blessing, I began to bless my son every night. I put my hand on his forehead and use the blessing that God gave Moses so that Aaron and the priests could bless the people. It's based on Numbers 6:24-26, and here's how I have prayed it over my son:

The Lord bless you and keep you. Make his face shine upon you and be gracious to you. The Lord turn his countenance to you and grant you peace. The Lord bless you—Father, Son, and Holy Spirit—and may you always know that you are a blessing.

My hope is that this will seep deep into his soul and some-where etched in his identity will be this unerasable truth: "You are *always* a blessing."

Over the years it was wonderful to see how important this bless-ing became to him. On nights when it was very late and time for nightly prayer, he would take my hand, put it on his forehead, and say, "Mom, just bless me." Other times, he would place his hand on my forehead and bless me. I, too, relished being blessed.

THE BLESSING OF SILENCE

Besides receiving the blessing from others, Fr. Nouwen says the most important place we receive the blessing is through prayer: "The real 'work' of prayer," he says, "is to become silent and lis-ten to the voice that says good things about me."[7] This is hard. We're afraid of silence because we're afraid we'll hear just the opposite—that we're no good; that no matter how hard we try, we'll just never measure up. For many of us, silence doesn't lead to blessing; it leads to shame. So in order to avoid encounter-ing the "critical parent," we avoid the silence. We go to prayer and we chatter like a chipmunk protecting her precious stash of shame-filled acorns.

Instead, Fr. Nouwen says, we have to silence the voices that question our goodness and trust that in silence, we will learn to hear again the voice of blessing. This is partly why prayer and Eucharistic adoration are so challenging and so important—because in the silence we can learn to hear again the voice of blessing. Fr. Nouwen reminds us: "It is not easy to enter into the silence and reach beyond the many boisterous and demanding voices of our world and to discover there the small intimate voice saying: 'You are my Beloved Child, on you my favor rests.'"[8]

At World Youth Day in Toronto, Canada, in July 2002, Pope John Paul II said something that struck all who heard it: "We are not the sum of our weaknesses and failures, we are the sum of the Father's love." I don't think John Paul II read that in a book. I think it emerged from his moments of silence before the Father, moments in which he experienced the Father's love and knew he was blessed.

Close your eyes for a moment and experience this reality: You are not the sum of your weaknesses and failures. You are the sum of the Father's love. He has chosen you. You are blessed. His Spirit rests on you.

Broken!

We are chosen, blessed, and then . . . broken. Darn! Why can't we just be chosen and blessed? Wouldn't that be so much better?

Fr. Nouwen has an incredibly insightful answer to that question. He says, "The way we are broken is as much an expression of our individuality as the way we are taken [chosen] and blessed."[9] In other words, the way I am broken tells you something unique about me. The way you are broken tells me something unique about you. Through the brokenness of my failed marriage, when the Lord told me I was "first a daughter, then a bride," he revealed that I was chosen, that my value came from my relationship with him and not from anything I do or accomplish. My brokenness became the gateway to deeper union with God and fashioned my unique fingerprints of suffering that define, in a distinctive way, who I am today.

Unfortunately, many people interpret their brokenness, pain, and suffering in the opposite way—as a confirmation that they are worthless, that they lack value. This was the common understanding of pain and suffering in Jesus' time. In John 9, as Jesus and his disciples are passing by a man born blind, the disciples ask, "Rabbi, who sinned, this man or his parents, that he was born blind?" (9:2). In other words, "Jesus, is this man suffering because of his own sin or that of his parents?" And Jesus responds: "Neither he nor his parents sinned; it is so that the works of God might be made visible through him" (9:3). The man's blindness is not because of his worthlessness or lack of value; rather, it is to let God's works show forth through him.

This is the most incredible thing about being broken—it's not supposed to destroy the blessing, but deepen it, to allow God to shine forth through us. Our brokenness, Fr. Nouwen says, is "an opportunity to purify and deepen the blessing that rests upon us."[10] What initially seemed like punishment or rejection is instead an invitation to deeper communion and dialogue with

God. It allows God's light to shine through you.

A woman was once asked by a co-worker, "What's it like to be a Christian?" The woman thought for a moment and said, "It is like being a pumpkin. God picks you from the patch, brings you in, and washes all the dirt off of you. Then he cuts off the top and scoops out all the yucky stuff. He removes the seeds of doubt, hate, and greed, and then he carves you a new smiling face and puts his light inside of you to shine for all the world to see."[11]

Jesus died on the cross so that God could scoop out all the "yucky" stuff—the bitterness, the self-loathing, the throttlehold of control—and carve a new life for you. God's mercy is precisely his redemptive ability to draw good out of evil, to bring his divine light into an otherwise suffocating darkness. Mercy, John Paul II says, is "love's second name,"[12] and it is "manifested in its true and proper aspect when it restores to value, promotes and draws good from all the forms of evil existing in the world and in man."[13] Through divine mercy, God transforms our brokenness into blessedness.

Isn't that precisely what we've seen throughout this book—that through the script changes of life, through being purified, carved, and broken, we find the path to deeper communion and intimacy with God, to even deeper blessedness? I'd like to go back to the Old Testament for a moment to the story of Ruth.

RUTH'S BROKENNESS

I love the story of Ruth. Ruth wasn't a Hebrew but a Moabite living in her native country. She probably dreamed of growing up and marrying a nice handsome Moabite man and settling down near her parents, grandparents, nieces, and nephews. But God had different plans. Naomi, the Hebrew, moved into town with her two bachelor sons, and Ruth was chosen and blessed to fall in love and marry one of Naomi's sons.

Ten years go by, and Ruth's husband dies. Naomi's husband dies. The other son dies, and the three widows are left childless. Naomi tells her daughters-in-law to go back to their families because she's moving to Israel. Right then, Ruth could have cut her losses and said, "Hasta la vista!" But she didn't. Instead, she said to Naomi some of the most beautiful verses in the Old Testament: "Wherever you go I will go, wherever you lodge I will lodge, your people shall be my people, and your God my God" (Ruth 1:16). Ruth pressed deeper into God instead of pulling away. She professed a heart of hope and patience, even when she couldn't see where the script change was taking her.

Ruth and Naomi return to Israel where they are the poorest of the poor—picking up the leftover grain in the field after the harvest. Ruth is poor, childless, a widow, and a foreigner. She is broken.

However, God is at work even when all observable evidence seemed to the contrary. Ruth meets her kinsman-in-law, Boaz; they marry, and she becomes the great-grandmother of King David. God was working . . . all the time, even though it was in a very hidden way, to bring about the fulfillment of his plan.

JOSEPH'S BROKENNESS

Joseph in the Old Testament was also chosen, blessed, and broken (see Genesis, chapters 37–50). He was chosen by his father as his favorite among his sons and given a distinctive coat of many colors. Joseph's blessing was confirmed by his dream in which the other sheaves of the field bowed down to Joseph's sheaf.

His brothers, however, didn't care too much for Joseph's blessedness. As a result, they dumped him into a well and sold him into slavery (sometimes betrayal hurts the most when it's from your own family, whether that's your natural family or your church family). Joseph found himself a slave in Egypt, where he was unjustly accused by Potiphar's wife and thrown into prison. Joseph went from being chosen and blessed to being broken.

While he was stuck in the muddy well, it would have been tempting for Joseph to think: "I guess I really deserved this. I did have those prideful dreams that exalted me above my brothers. This is just a confirmation that I'm no good and never should have been born." And again while he was in Pharaoh's prison for many years, he could have thought: "Well, obviously God doesn't care about me because if he did, he wouldn't have allowed this to happen a second time!"

I don't think these were his thoughts, and here's why. First, that's not the way God works. He doesn't smash us down in our shame. And second, because if Joseph had thought in that way, he wouldn't have had the confidence and character to become the second most powerful man in all of Egypt. God used Joseph's brokenness, not to confirm his worthlessness, but to affirm his belovedness, that he was chosen by God even if the circumstances appeared to the contrary. Divine mercy was at work to draw good out of evil.

Over the years, Joseph endured the pain and suffering; he endured his brokenness, waiting for God's promise to be fulfilled. He walked the way of the cross, not away from the cross, and eventually his suffering bore tremendous fruit. Joseph was raised to Pharaoh's right hand, and when a famine hit the land of Israel and his brothers came to him for food, Joseph was ready. When God's timing was right, Joseph was in a position for God's plan to be fulfilled through him. And notice what he told his brothers: "Even though you meant harm to me, God meant it for good, to achieve his present end, the survival of many people" (Genesis 50:20). That's a heart of hope and patience that believes God works everything together for the good. Joseph actively waited in the present moment, full of the conviction that something was happening right where he was, even if that was in prison. He trusted so deeply that his waiting was open to all possibilities.[14] He believed in divine mercy.

ABRAHAM'S BROKENNESS

Abraham, too, was chosen and blessed—to be the father of many nations. But he was also broken. He received the promise at age seventy-five. Isaac, as we saw before, was born when Abraham was one hundred (see Genesis 12:4; 17:17). Now I'm not terrific at math, but even I can figure out that's twenty-five long years of waiting for the promise to be fulfilled, twenty-five years of being broken.

Why did God tarry? To toy with Abraham? To delight in making him a pawn in an intergalactic chess game? Never! He tarried to purify the blessing that rested upon Abraham and to let the works of God be made visible through him. (When Isaac was born, don't you think it was pretty obvious that God had something to do with it?)

Given!

However, there's one last movement in the Eucharistic pattern. Thank goodness we don't end at being broken. We are chosen, blessed, broken, and *given*. Our brokenness is what allows us to be given in a particular way, to fulfill the unique mission that God has for our lives. Joseph's brokenness allowed him to be given as second in command in all of Egypt and as the one who would save the Hebrew people from starvation. Abraham's brokenness allowed him to be given as the father of all the nations, our father in faith. Ruth's brokenness allowed her to be given to her kinsman Boaz in marriage and to become the great-grandmother of King David.

And Mary's life, too, followed the Eucharistic pattern. She was chosen—chosen as the Mother of God; blessed—"blessed is the fruit of your womb" (Luke 1:42); broken—"a sword will pierce your own soul" (Luke 2:35, NRSV); and given—at the foot of the cross, "Woman, behold, your son . . . . Behold, your mother" (John 19:26-27). Mary's brokenness at the foot of the cross is precisely why she is given to us, because she is totally poured out and available to be our mother, not for her own benefit, but to let God's works be made visible through her. She is our Mother of Divine Mercy.

In my own life, in your own life, the unique way we have been broken is directly linked to the unique way in which we are to be given, to our unique mission. No one can be given in exactly the same way you can. The reason I am an author and retreat speaker today is not because of my great talents but because of my brokenness. The gift you have to give to the Church and the world is not because of your great talents but because of your brokenness. Here's a favorite story of mine that illustrates this point:

A water bearer in India had two large pots. Each pot hung on the end of a pole, which the servant carried across his neck. One of the pots had a crack in it; and while the other pot was perfect and always delivered a full portion of water at the end of the long walk from the stream to the master's house, the cracked pot arrived only half full. For two years this went on daily, with the servant delivering only one and a half pots of water to his master's house. Of course, the perfect pot was proud of its accomplishments, perfect for the end for which it was made.

But the poor cracked pot was ashamed of its own imperfection, and miserable that it was able to accomplish only half of what it had been made to do. After two years of what it perceived to be a bitter failure, it spoke to the water bearer one day by the stream. "I am ashamed of myself, and I want to apologize to you."

"Why?" asked the bearer. "What are you ashamed of?"

The pot replied, "I have been able, for these past two years, to deliver only half my load, because this crack in my side causes water to leak out all the way back to your master's house. Because of my flaws, you have to do all of this work, and you don't get full value from your efforts."

The water bearer felt sorry for the old cracked pot, and in his compassion he said, "As we return to the master's house, I want you to notice the beautiful flowers along the path."

Indeed, as they went up the hill, the old cracked pot took notice of the sun warming the beautiful wildflowers on the side of the path, and this cheered it some. But at the end of the trail, it still felt badly because it had leaked out half its load, and so again it apologized to the bearer for its failure.

The bearer said to the pot, "Did you notice that there were flowers only on your side of the path, but not on the other pot's side? That's because I have always known about your flaw, and I took advantage of it. I planted flower seeds on your side of the path, and every day while we walked back from the stream, you watered them. For two years I have been able to pick these beautiful flowers to decorate my master's table. Without you being just the way you are, he would not have this beauty to grace his house."[15]

Like the cracked pot, how harshly we judge our imperfections! And yet, also like the cracked pot, the gift you have to give to the world is not because of your perfection, but because of your brokenness.

There's a moving song by Christian musician Mark Schultz that captures this idea so well. It's called "Broken and Beautiful,"[16] and the words expose the rawness of life, but like the cracked pot, they remind us to experience the beauty of our brokenness:

Well he's never been to church before / But he came today as a last resort / the world was caving in / And he was suffocating in his sin / But tears rolled down / As hope rushed in / He closed his eyes / Raised his hands / Worshipping the God who can / Bring him back to life again.

It's beautiful / Beautiful / Come as you are / Surrender your heart / Broken and beautiful / Cause there's nothing more beautiful to God / Than when his sons and daughters come / Broken . . . Broken and beautiful.

A friend of mine, Pat, wrestled with God for years over her brokenness. The script of her life changed dramatically in 1975 with the birth of her daughter, Jennifer. Like many expectant parents, Pat and her husband talked about their dreams for their daughter and their anticipated script: she would be beautiful, smart, and happy. Although there were serious complications during the birth, mother and daughter made it through, and all seemed well.

However, their daughter was radically delayed in reaching the developmental milestones all parents watch for, such as sitting up, crawling, and walking. Eventually, Jennifer was diagnosed with mild to moderate mental retardation and neurological damage. School became a nightmare, and innocent questions from Jennifer like "Mommy, will I have disabilities in heaven?" tore at Pat's heart.

Over the years, God's different plan became apparent, but that didn't make it easy for Pat to accept. She wondered why this had happened, what she had done wrong, and especially how she could make it go away and make her daughter "normal." Pat admits, "I didn't like God's version of the script of my life or my daughter's life. I wanted us to be like everyone else—but we were blessed and chosen to be a little different."

As Jennifer grew into a teenager, Pat often marveled that her daughter was never angry with God. Jennifer never blamed him for her troubles. When her daughter developed very bad acne, Pat railed against God: "I remember driving down the highway, talking out loud, saying, 'Really, God, acne too? Where's the fairness in that? Lighten up, already!'" Of course, the acne didn't immediately disappear, but later that day, a friend called Pat to tell her about a new treatment. "God is good, and he is listening," Pat says. "The trick for me is to also be listening."

In 2004, Pat and her family moved to Phoenix, Arizona, where she anticipated lots of year-round golf and relaxation. However, she quickly discovered there were no activities for Jennifer in the area. Pat got together with another mother and started a Special Olympics program. Currently, over forty adults compete in four to five sports per year. "It's a lot of work," Pat acknowledges, "but wow, the inspiration!"

Over the years, Pat slowly allowed—and accepted—the Eucharistic pattern to be inscribed in her life. Her brokenness is precisely how she is now given—not only to her daughter, but to over forty other adults and their families. As she reflects on her life, she concludes:

Script changes don't always seem to be good at the time. However, I have learned to try to be patient and to accept that while I don't have to understand God's plan, I do have to live it. I have been blessed time and time again in ways I certainly would never have chosen for myself. Sometimes, I even get a chance to look back on the changes that seemed horrible at the time and to see the good that came from them. Those moments give me the strength to get through the times when I don't understand. Scripts do change, but God's love for us never does.

St. Paul encountered numerous hardships and script changes in his efforts to preach the gospel. And yet, he allowed the Eucharistic pattern to underwrite all he did. He reminds the Corinthians that his sufferings are for *their* encouragement; he is "broken and given" so that they can draw hope from God's faithfulness to him. It may be worth underlining these verses in your Bible:

Blessed be the God and Father of our Lord Jesus Christ, the Father of compassion and God of all encouragement, who encourages us in our every affliction, so that we may be able to encourage those who are in any affliction with the encouragement with which we ourselves are encouraged by God. For as Christ's sufferings overflow to us, so through Christ does our encouragement also overflow. If we are afflicted, it is for your encouragement and salvation; if we are encouraged, it is for your encouragement, which enables you to endure the same sufferings that we suffer. Our hope for you is firm, for we know that as you share in the sufferings, you also share in the encouragement. (2 Corinthians 1:3-7)

In his chapter on brokenness, Fr. Nouwen describes a striking scene from Leonard Bernstein's *Mass* (a musical work written for the opening of the John F. Kennedy Center for the Performing Arts in Washington, D.C.). Here's Fr. Nouwen's description of the musical tribute:

Toward the end of this work, the priest, richly dressed in splendid liturgical vestments, is lifted up by his people. He towers high above the adoring crowd, carrying in his hands a glass chalice. Suddenly, the human pyramid collapses, and the priest comes tumbling down. His vestments are ripped off, and his glass chalice falls to the ground and is shattered. As he walks slowly through the debris of his former glory—barefoot, wearing only blue jeans and a T-shirt—children's voices are heard singing, "Laude, laude, laude"—"Praise, praise, praise." Suddenly the priest notices the broken chalice. He looks at it for a long time and then, haltingly, he says, "I never realized that broken glass could shine so brightly."[17]

"I never realized that broken glass could shine so brightly." Why was the man born blind? To let God's glory shine through. Why was Jesus Christ nailed to the cross? To let God's glory shine through. Why do you experience brokenness in your life? Not to crush you in your worthlessness but to raise you up so that you can shine so brightly with a light that does not come from you but from the Eucharistic pattern inscribed in your life. Like a stained glass window that allows the sun to stream through, you are created for God's glory to shine through you!

The Gift of Death

Toward the end of *Life of the Beloved*, Fr. Nouwen makes one final connection between brokenness and gift. He says we are called to give ourselves not only in life but in death. Death, which is our final brokenness, is to become the means to our final gift of self. Here's how Fr. Nouwen summarizes this truth: "For those who know that they are chosen, blessed, and broken to be given, dying is the way to becoming pure gift."[18]

Dying is the way to becoming pure gift. Death is our final act of giving. I once heard death described as putting out the lamp because the dawn has come. Death doesn't extinguish your gift of self; it releases your gift of self. We are called not only to live for others but to die for others. This is why St. Thérèse of Lisieux said that she wanted to spend her heaven doing good on earth. She knew that the brokenness of death was the gateway to eternal self-giving. She wasn't going to heaven to join a club of saints that played cards and croquet all day, but to be part of the communion of saints, the eternal self-giving of those who know they are chosen, blessed, and broken to be given for others.

But you know and I know that we experience many little deaths every day—when your husband seems oblivious to your fatigue and sacrifice, when your thirteen-year-old daughter tells you she watched an R-rated movie at a slumber party, when your room-mate leaves the dishes in the sink. It's so important that we don't waste these little deaths. A college-aged friend of mine worked at a summer camp for kids a couple of years ago, and when I asked her how it was going, she said, "We came here to die!" So true! They were learning how to die to self and give at the same time. The same invitation is offered to us. Instead of closing in and hardening out hearts, we should allow these little (and big) deaths to open our hearts, to spur us on to deeper self-giving, to practice dying and giving, dying and giving, so that when we finally do die, it should be the most natural thing to die and give of ourselves at the same time.

Praying the Eucharistic Pattern

Chosen, blessed, broken, and given. This is the pattern for our lives and for our prayer—to go to God and say:

"Thank you that I am chosen, that I am your daughter, your beloved. Thank you that you love me, that you have selected me, that you love my person, not my performance.

"Thank you that I am blessed among women, that when I come into your presence, I hear words of blessing, not words of shame and condemnation. Thank you, Father, that I am not the sum of my weaknesses and failures, but the sum of your love. Help me to know that I am always a blessing even when I don't feel like it.

"Thank you that I am broken. Thank you for all the script changes in my life. Thank you for the times when life doesn't go my way. Thank you for all the saints and examples in the Bible of people who were broken and so let God's glory shine through. Help me to let your glory shine through my brokenness. Help me to believe that you are working even when I can't see it. Help me to trust in your divine mercy."

And finally,

"Thank you that I am given. Thank you that the way I am broken is directly linked to the way I am given—to my family, my friends, the Church, and the world. Help me to be given more. Help me to hold nothing back. Help me to be willing to be broken more so that I can be given more. Lord, I give you permission: take me, bless me, break me, and give me as Eucharist to the world."

This is how the Eucharistic pattern becomes inscribed in our lives and becomes the pattern for our prayer, so that every time we go to Mass and hear the priest say, "Jesus took the bread, blessed it, broke it, and gave it to his disciples, saying, 'Take this all of you and eat it. This is my body given up for you,'" our hearts will leap and say, "Yes, Father, I want that to be me. I want to be chosen, blessed, broken, and given. I want to be Eucharist in the world. Let me live the Eucharistic pattern every day of my life and fulfill the unique mission you have for me."

The Eucharist is indeed the greatest gift that God has ever given to mankind. The Eucharist shows us that it wasn't enough for God to die on the cross, rise from the dead, and send the Holy Spirit. He also wanted to remain among us forever. He wanted to be with us . . . all the time, because God is Love, and Love wants to be with the beloved forever. This is the divine mystery of Love that our lives need to be anchored in, especially when life doesn't go the way we want.

Questions for Reflection and Discussion:

1. What thoughts or ideas struck you in this chapter?

2. How have you experienced being chosen in a human way, such as by winning a contest, being chosen for a coveted job, or being chosen by your spouse? How have you experienced being chosen by God?

3. Do you experience being blessed in your life by others, or do you experience an "affirmation desert"?

4. If you could ask someone to do something to "bless you" (to help you feel cherished), what would it be?

5. Do you see a link between the way you have been broken and the way you are able to give of yourself to God and others? Please explain.

6. After reading this chapter, what are your thoughts about death?

7. Go back and pray again the four movements of the Eucharistic pattern, letting each one sink deep into your being.

CHAPTER 5

THE DIVINE MARINADE

A few summers ago, I stayed with some dear friends in Denver, Colorado. As we sat down to dinner, they offered me a steak. Now, I don't really like steak because it's usually not very tasty, but I took one bite and my taste buds exploded for joy. It was so good. It was so tender. It had so much taste. What was the secret? The marinade.

As we've been discovering, the secret of navigating the script changes in life is not to demand that God answer our prayers our way, but to cultivate the eyes of faith and a heart of hope (and patience) that says, "God is good . . . all the time. God is working . . . all the time. God is with us . . . all the time." In other words, to remind ourselves that God is working, even when all evidence is to the contrary and we can't see his plan. Likewise, we need to remember that brokenness is not designed to crush us in our weakness, but to purify the blessing that rests upon us so that we can be given even more.

That's why I like to think of the context for our everyday life as the "Divine Marinade." It's what we bathe our hearts in. It's something we work at, but it's also something we rest in. A good steak doesn't think, "Okay, I've got to work really hard to sit in this marinade." Instead, it just sits there and lets the marinade do its thing.

The purpose of a good marinade is to make the meat tender, to break down the tough fibers. So, too, the purpose of the Divine Marinade is to make our hearts tender, to break down the tough fibers, so that when life doesn't go our way or we experience being broken, we don't harden our hearts; instead they remain soft and tender and open to the love of God and others.

Detachment

So what's the first ingredient in the Divine Marinade? It's detachment. Detachment helps to bathe our hearts and break down the fibers of *attachment* because attachments cause our hearts to cling to other things and people. They're often what cause our hearts to harden and resist God.

There's a well-known saint who could have easily taken his heart out of the Divine Marinade and let it become hardened because of the unjust circumstances of his life. This saint was kidnapped by his own Carmelite order, locked away in a prison, and given starvation rations. I'm speaking of St. John of the Cross.

Fr. Iain Matthews, the author of a wonderful book on St. John of the Cross called *Impact of God*, explains what St. John means by detachment (what the saint also calls *nada*—nothingness): it's a kind of emptiness. It's the empty space God has to create within us so he can fill it. In the spiritual life, Fr. Matthew says, the key word is not so much "achievement" as "space."[1]

This can be hard for Westerners to hear because we usually measure how spiritual we are by how much we achieve, by how many things we check off our spiritual checklist. But John of the Cross says our progress in the spiritual life is measured not so much by how much ground we cover but by the amount of room God is given to maneuver.[2] God is a big God. He needs lots of space within us to dwell. The Gospel of John says, "Whoever loves me will keep my word, and my Father will love him, and we will come to him and make our dwelling with him" (John 14:23).

Do you remember the old joke, "Where does a two-ton elephant sit?" Answer: "Anywhere he wants." Here's the spiritual equivalent: "How much space does God take up?" Answer: "As much space as he can get."

Stripping Away Attachments

However, most of us don't voluntarily remove our attachments and create more room for God. Our hearts aren't empty stables; they're stuffed closets. As a result, we don't usually jump to the front of the line and say, "Pick me! Pick me! Create an empty space within me!" Most of us tend to be line slinkers. We slink to the back of the line and hope God won't notice us; we hope God will stay occupied stripping away someone else's attachments rather than our own.

I hate to break the news to you: line slinking may work for a while, but eventually God turns his loving attention to us, and then watch out! He allows suffering or a script change to come our way because suffering can do for us what we can't do on our own. It hollows us out. It strips away our attachments. It creates space within us. This is why the saints welcomed suffering. They realized it was a crucial ingredient in the Divine Marinade—to soften and detach their hearts in a way they couldn't accomplish on their own.

For many years, my image of Christian detachment was of someone who was unemotional, someone who rose above the circumstances so that nothing affected them. Their emotional EKG would look like a straight line with almost no change.

A conversation with someone in this detached mode might go like this: "Would you like to go to lunch?" "Oh, I don't care." "Where would you like to go?" "You know, it really doesn't matter to me." "Well, then, would you like steak or fish?" (Smiling) "You know, I really don't have a preference. Either is fine with me. Why don't you decide?"

I don't know about you, but I just want to throttle that person! I want to say, "Hello! Anyone in there? Would you please come back down to earth and put your humanity on again!" We're not angels; we're human beings. God created each of us uniquely with preferences, opinions, likes, and dislikes. My son loves basketball; I cared little about it until he started playing the game. I love to dance tango; my son thinks it's the most tedious thing in the world.

But here's the tricky part: how do we acknowledge that God made us with likes and dislikes and yet not allow these preferences to dominate us, to take up space within us and so crowd out God?

EMBRACING THE OUTCOME WITH PASSION

The answer, I believe, is passion. Surprised? I was. You see, what bothered me about ultra-spiritual detachment is that it leaves no place for passion. When I read the gospels, I see that Christ was a passionate person. He calmed the sea with passion. (Can you imagine Jesus saying to the waves, "You know, it would be really *nice* if you kind of calmed down and took a little nap"? I don't think so.) He wept at Lazarus' tomb with passion. He reproached Peter with passion.

Jesus wasn't indifferent to carrying his cross. He carried it with passion. And Mary, too, was passionate. She said yes to the angel with passion, she lived a hidden life in Nazareth with passion, and she wept at the cross with passion.

And what about you and me? I'm a passionate person, you're a passionate person, we're all passionate. What I realized is that detachment isn't strangling our passion so that we have no emotion and are indifferent to whatever happens. Detachment is embracing the outcome of a situation with passion, whether it's A or B. So, if A happens, I win. If B happens, I win, and whether it's A or B, I embrace it *with passion.*

Does this sound a bit abstract? Well, then, let's make it more concrete. I love chocolate ice cream. My son loves vanilla. Here's the scenario: we go into a store and can only buy one kind of ice cream to share. Does detachment mean that suddenly a wave of the Holy Spirit washes over me, and like a robot, I no longer care whether we get chocolate or vanilla? No, I still love chocolate, but I ask the Holy Spirit to help me find joy whether we get A or B. If we get chocolate, I win, and if we get vanilla, I win. The Holy Spirit is helping to strip away my attachment that makes me think I will *only* be happy if I get chocolate.

Maybe you don't love ice cream, so let's try another example. Let's say you have an appointment at 3:00 p.m., and on the way you encounter lots of red lights and heavy traffic. When you arrive at 3:35 p.m., is your heart resting in the Divine Marinade, all calm and collected? Why not? Why is it that we experience joy and satisfaction if we're on time and frustration and anger if we're late? Detachment says we win if we're on time and we win if we're late, because our joy and peace come not from the gratification of being on time, but from creating more space within us for God, whether A or B happens.

Let me give one final example using St. Francis of Assisi's explanation of perfect joy, which he gave to Br. Leo:

If, when we shall arrive at St. Mary of the Angels [monastery], all drenched with rain and trembling with cold, all covered with mud and exhausted from hunger; if, when we knock at the convent-gate, the porter should come angrily and ask us who we are; if, after we have told him, "We are two of the brethren," he should answer angrily, "What ye say is not the truth; ye are but two impostors going about to deceive the world, and take away the alms of the poor; begone I say"; if then he refuse to open to us, and leave us outside, exposed to the snow and rain, suffering from cold and hunger till nightfall—then, if we accept such injustice, such cruelty and such contempt with patience, without being ruffled and without murmuring, believing with humility and charity that the porter really knows us, and that it is God who maketh him to speak thus against us, write down, O Brother Leo, that this is perfect joy.

And if we knock again, and the porter come out in anger to drive us away with oaths and blows, as if we were vile impostors, saying, 'Begone, miserable robbers! to the hospital, for here you shall neither eat nor sleep!—and if we accept all this with patience, with joy, and with charity, O Brother Leo, write that this indeed is perfect joy.

And if, urged by cold and hunger, we knock again, calling to the porter and entreating him with many tears to open to us and give us shelter, for the love of God, and if he come out more angry than before, exclaiming, "These are but importunate rascals, I will deal with them as they deserve"; and taking a knotted stick, he seize us by the hood, throwing us on the ground, rolling us in the snow, and shall beat and wound us with the knots in the stick—if we bear all these injuries with patience and joy, thinking of the sufferings of our Blessed Lord, which we would share out of love for him, write, O Brother Leo, that here, finally, is perfect joy.[3]

Why is this perfect joy? Because if "A" had happened, if they had been let into the monastery, they would have embraced it with passion and found joy. And if "B" had happened, if they were turned away and were rejected and beaten, they would have embraced it with passion and found joy. Francis' heart was open to the will of God either way.

You see, detachment is *not* seeking the most unappealing choice and assuming that because it's unappealing, it must be God's will. No, detachment is living and embracing life with passion, whether A happens or B happens, whether you have six children or no children, whether you're in a relationship or not, whether they let you into the monastery or throw you out. And when we live this way, then we become free—free to create more space within us for God, free to draw closer to God through prayer, no matter what the outcome. Here's how one saying expresses it: Happiness is being able to enjoy the scenery, even on a detour.

Consecration

What about the second ingredient in the Divine Marinade? It's consecration, and this ingredient can be a bit bitter and, in fact, even prompt tears, much like an onion.

Now, you may remember that I was born and raised in San Diego, which is the last beach town in California before Mexico. That means I love the sun, the ocean, and the beach. However, for more than twenty-three years, I lived in Ohio, which meant no ocean, no beach, and not a lot of sun or warmth from November to April. Bermuda, on the other hand, is nestled in the sun and warmth of the Atlantic Ocean. Now, if I had my choice, do you think I'd rather be in Ohio or Bermuda in the month of March? Bermuda, naturally.

Well, several years ago, I was invited to go to Bermuda to give a retreat for women, and as you can imagine, I was happy to say, "Oh yes, *fiat*, let it be done unto me according to thy word!"

However, some awkward miscommunication occurred via e-mail, and one day the retreat organizers informed me they would get back to me as to whether they still wanted me to come. In the meantime, guess who had to practice detachment? Me. I had to say I would find joy if I went to Bermuda, and I would also find joy if I stayed home. Well, they cancelled my trip, and I wasn't very joyful or detached about it. In fact, I found it very difficult to deal with the "loss" of Bermuda. I was upset at God because I didn't understand why he gave it to me only to take it away. I felt like God was toying with me. Why did he give it to me in the first place?

Offering Everything Back to God

Oh, but there was such an important lesson to be learned in the midst of this that was absolutely worth not going to Bermuda. God taught me that he gives us things precisely so that we can *offer it back*. If God didn't give me anything, I would have to come to him empty-handed. I wouldn't have anything to offer back to him. Instead, he gave me Bermuda; and I willingly received it. Not only did I receive it, but I anticipated all the sun and warmth and emotional delight it would bring me. But Bermuda wasn't mine to keep. He gave Bermuda to me so that I could offer it back to him, sacrifice it back to him.

I would imagine this reminds you of someone in the Old Testament we've already mentioned: Abraham. It's no wonder he's called our father in faith! He shows us how to respond when life doesn't go our way—how to be chosen, blessed, broken, and given—and he shows us the meaning of consecration.

Sometimes I wish I could hop in a time machine and go back to when Abraham was walking toward the mountain to sacrifice Isaac and listen in on his thoughts. He had to be wondering, "God, you are really a crazy God. Here I wait twenty-five years to have this son, and now you ask me to sacrifice him back to you? I don't get it. Why didn't you just keep him in the first place?"

But Abraham was learning the meaning of consecration. He was learning that consecration is offering back to God that which we possess, that which he has given to us. That's what Abraham learned, and that's what I was learning through Bermuda—to *offer it back*.

But please notice: we can't consecrate what we don't possess. I can't consecrate my friend's Mercedes-Benz convertible to God. I don't own it; I don't possess it; I can't offer it back. But I can consecrate the baby in my womb, or the house I own, or the job I go to day after day, or the depression I'm experiencing, or the family tension that exasperates me.

One of the most common cries I hear from women who have had miscarriages or who experience the early death of a child is this: Why did God give me this baby only to take the child away? The answer is: consecration. God is inviting you to consecrate that child to him because you really did possess it—your womb enclosed it—and so you can offer that child's life back to God. It wasn't a waste. It wasn't a mistake. And most of all, *it wasn't a punishment*. It was an invitation to consecration.

I recently experienced this invitation to consecration in a very profound and public way through the Cosentino family. Upon their fifth miscarriage, Steve and Bridgette Cosentino invited family and friends to a burial service. Rather than hiding their grief from their five children and others, they spoke of offering their child back to God. In response, their eldest, Angela, then fifteen years old, composed the following poem, written from the point of view of her unborn sibling:

A Letter to My Family

To Mom and Dad, brothers and sisters too,
You all should know my greatest love for you.
And though I am on earth, alas, no longer,
The presence of my spirit is much stronger.

A Trinitarian love from husband to wife
Bursts forth a child, the greatest gift of life.
And in the womb I was conceived so small
Yet never had I the chance to grow too tall.

My first and smallest step I did not take.
A single word of sound I did not make.
I wasn't ever able to laugh or cry,
Yet now I say my very dearest good-bye.

I wish I could have known you here on earth.
You've recognized my value and my worth.
You hold my precious life close to your heart,
Yet sadly from this world I had to part.

My name comes from John Paul the Great, our Pope.
He fills our lives with a love for life and hope.
I thank you for your openness to me,
For now it is the angels and saints I see.

Oh, what a joy it is to simply lie
In company of our Lord in the sky!
I intercede for you each night and day,
That you might join the five of us, I pray.

And then our glorious family shall unite!
I cannot wait to see this splendid sight!

Consecration not only kept the hearts of the parents open, but
it also kept the hearts of their children open to God and to his
will. Like detachment, consecration doesn't latch onto something
and make it the source of my happiness and fulfillment. It keeps
offering everything back to God.

In my speaking ministry, I have to exercise consecration constantly. Bermuda was just the first instance. Another time I was
asked in the spring to give a retreat for women on Long Island,
New York, on the tenth of November. Two months later, the
retreat organizers e-mailed me and said they were postponing
the retreat for another time, because they wanted to make it a
weekend retreat and not just one day. I was disappointed, but I
offered it back to God.

A week or so later, I received an e-mail asking me to appear on a Catholic television show on November 8. I thought, "Oh, God, *now* I get it. You cancelled the Long Island retreat so that I could be available for this show." Happily I bought my plane ticket and informed the show's producer of my travel arrangements. The next day, the producer returned my call with some surprising news: there was a new host for this show, and the take-over date for the new host was . . . November 8. Additionally, the new host had already booked someone for that date so they would get back to me another time.

Consecration, consecration. "Offer it back, offer it back," I kept telling myself. Then in late September, a friend of mine from Maryland called. She was organizing a retreat for women and wanted me to be a speaker. I cringed as I asked her the date because my fall calendar was really booked. Guess what date her retreat was? November 9–11. And because of the two previous cancellations, it was wide open. "Oh, God, now I *really* get why the other two booked and cancelled. It was so that this date would be open for this retreat! Thank you, thank you, Lord. You are so merciful."

And that's precisely what happened: I gave the retreat in Maryland in which I spoke about . . . life not going the way you want.

I really love consecration because it helps my heart to stay pliable. In some ways, consecration is yoga for the soul. It stretches us and helps our hearts to stay supple and elastic when we're tempted to draw in and become bitter, especially when other people's choices affect us without *our* consent.

Spiritual Virginity

The final ingredient in the Divine Marinade is what makes it all sweet, kind of like honey. It's virginity, or rather, spiritual virginity. Now I would imagine that you didn't expect to read about virginity in this book, and I certainly never expected to be speaking and writing about it, but allow me to tell you how spiritual virginity came to be part of the Divine Marinade of my life.

On December 8, 1999, the feast of the Immaculate Conception, I spent most of the day meditating on Mary's virginity. This, in turn, led me to think about how we could talk to teens about chastity and virginity in a way that wouldn't evoke the eye-rolling, "I've-heard-it-all-before, let's-count-the-dots-on-the-ceiling" response, but instead would rock their world with the same head-rushing enthusiasm as zooming to the top of the Eiffel Tower.

A POSITIVE DEFINITION OF VIRGINITY

However, the biggest problem in talking about virginity today is that almost no one talks about it. And I think the reason is because we have the wrong definition. If I asked one hundred people, "What's a virgin?" I would get the same answer one hundred times: "Someone who hasn't had sex." This is a severely inadequate definition because it tells us only what a virgin is *not*.

It would be like telling a child that a dog isn't a cat, or a rose isn't a wheelbarrow. These are negative definitions; they say what something isn't. But I wanted a positive definition of virginity. I wanted to know what a virgin *is*. So how do we go about creating this positive definition of virginity?

These were my thoughts as I drove from New York City to Ohio in January of 2000 with nothing to do for eight hours but ponder virginity. About five hours into the drive, it hit me: virginity doesn't have to do with sexual relations *per se* but with union. Virginity is the physical, emotional, and spiritual capacity for infinite and undiminishable union. And, of course, this capacity for total and complete union is expressed perfectly in God.

My brain chugged away trying to keep multiple windows open on the desktop of my mind as I worked to wrap my mind around virginity *in* God. If God the Father is perfectly virginal, that means that no matter how much he unites himself with someone or something, that union is infinite and undiminishable. Virginity in God isn't a state of the body that can be "lost." It's a divine attribute. It's part of God's essence. To be God is to be virgin—to have the capacity for infinite and undiminishable union.

But then I asked myself, with whom does the "virgin" Father enter into infinite and undiminishable union? With the Son, of course. But the Son is also God. That means he's the "virgin" Son, and so he can enter into infinite and undiminishable union with the Father. And here's the best part: the union between the Father and Son is not sterile but fruitful. The infinite and undiminishable union between the Father and Son bursts forth in another person—the Holy Spirit, the "virgin" Spirit. Virginity within the Trinity isn't sterile but fruitful, fertile.

As I sped past the hills of Pennsylvania, my mind raced to new insights about the Trinity. In the Trinity, virginity, union, and fruitfulness are inseparable. Divine virginity doesn't exist apart from union, and divine union doesn't exist apart from fruitfulness. The three are always intertwined like three strands of the divine cord of Love.[4]

I know these thoughts about the Trinity can be a bit off-putting when you first encounter them. Our society is so accustomed to thinking about virginity as having to do with sexual relations that it can be disturbing to try to apply this category of thinking to God. But take heart! This whole book has been an invitation to change our categories of thinking, to change the way we view brokenness, pain, and suffering. This is another milestone on that journey. I am asking you to delete the societal definition of virginity and replace it with a theological one—that virginity is the capacity in God for infinite and undiminishable union. Ironically, this is precisely what we confess every Sunday in the Creed when we say, "I believe in *one* God." We are saying: I believe in a God who is three distinct Persons but who is also mysteriously one because the union between them is perfect, complete, infinite, and undiminishable—in a word, virginal.

Having spent time in the heart of the Trinity, there was still one more step to go. I needed to bring these insights down to earth by asking: how does this apply to me? I'm certainly not infinite or undiminishable, yet I am made in the image and likeness of God. That means that somehow divine virginity is inscribed in my being. But how? How does virginity make the translation from the divine level to the human level?

Totally Available for Union

The Holy Spirit must have been working overtime because the answer tumbled into my mind: virginity, on the human level, is being totally available for union. That was it! I'd found it! I'd found the positive definition of virginity: being totally available for union. It's hard to put on a two-dimensional page the impact of this three-dimensional statement. I could no longer look at virginity as merely a physical state and therefore dismiss it as "DNA"—does not apply to me. If virginity is also the *spiritual* quality of being totally available for union with God, then every person, including me, is called to spiritual virginity. There are no exceptions, no exemptions. We're all called to be virgins!

I said this last statement once at a very large family conference in England, and I could see intrigue, fear, and confusion simultaneously cross the participants' faces. I laughed and said,

"If you're married, turn to your spouse and say, 'Honey, I want to be married to you and live the virginal life.'" Living the virginal life for married people doesn't mean giving up the beautiful gift of sexual intimacy with their spouse. In fact, it means just the opposite. Living the virginal life means we become aware of those things in our life that increase our ability for union—increase our ability to live holiness and sacrifice for the good of others (including our spouse)—as well as those things that detract or even destroy our ability to live for union.

When we become aware of the profound meaning of virginity and its positive definition as applying to every one of us, our entire life receives a new alignment, kind of like a spiritual chiropractic adjustment. We begin to realize that we can take back the territory that we've unwillingly ceded to a wrong definition. Suddenly everything, *everything*, becomes an invitation to grow in virginity, to grow in our ability to be totally available for union with God and others.

In my own life, I started begging God to make me totally available for union, and soon even mundane tasks took on new savor. Folding laundry, washing dishes, writing articles, playing softball with my son, and teaching swing dancing all became opportunities to cultivate within me the quality of being totally available for union. Inconveniences, irritations, humiliations, and changed scripts became the means to remove the obstacles for union. Why?

Because the virginal life, as with everything truly human, is based on the profound integration between body and spirit. God designed the body to perfectly express the spirit, to be the perfect means by which we give ourselves away in (virginal) love. Thus, every activity, thought, relationship, movie, or even a changed script either increases the body-spirit integration or ruptures it. It either helps body and spirit work together for union, or it pits the body and spirit against each other—and we give in to addictions, dismiss the goodness of God, or pretend that our bodies don't exist or aren't important.

Perhaps the difference between a great cell-phone connection and a dropped call can illustrate the body-spirit relationship. A great cell-phone connection keeps the communication flowing; a dropped call completely interrupts it. Of course, there's always the third option of a poor connection, where you strain to hear the other person and only catch intermittent words. This may be a more apt description of the body-spirit connection in our culture, where sometimes the body and spirit work together and sometimes the connection is fuzzy.

Using this imagery, we can say that the virginal life and everything that contributes to it is the perfect, crystal clear, continuous connection between body and spirit so that we remain connected (united) to God's love (and even increase our capacity for receiving it), and thus become a clear channel of God's love to others (union with others). It's like having a five-bar connection all the time!

I can remember reading one day about St. Thérèse of Lisieux and how she agonized to find her vocation in life. One day she cried out in ecstasy because she had finally discovered it: "My vocation," she said, "is love!" When I discovered spiritual virginity, I wanted to do the same thing. I wanted to shout out: "I have finally found my vocation. My vocation is to live the virginal life—to be totally available for union with God!"

SCRIPTURAL IMAGERY OF GOD AS SPOUSE

Scripture is full of this bridal imagery concerning us and God. One of the most eloquent passages is Hosea 2:21-22: "I will espouse you to me forever: / I will espouse you in right and in justice, / in love and in mercy; / I will espouse you in fidelity, / and you shall know the LORD." And Isaiah 54:5: "For he who has become your husband is your Maker; / his name is the LORD of hosts; / Your redeemer is the Holy One of Israel, / called God of all the earth."

In Ephesians, St. Paul connects the bridal relationship between man and wife with Christ's love for the Church: "'For this reason a man shall leave (his) father and (his) mother and be joined to his wife, and the two shall become one flesh.' [Paul is quoting Genesis 2:24.] This is a great mystery, but I speak in reference to Christ and the church" (5:31-32). God is not only Father to us, but he goes a step further to become Spouse.

This nuptial imagery reaches its crescendo in the Book of Revelation, where St. John first hears the shouts of a great crowd who cry: "Alleluia! / The Lord has established his reign, / [our]

God, the almighty. / Let us rejoice and be glad / and give him glory. / For the wedding day of the Lamb has come, / his bride has made herself ready" (19:6-7). And again, almost at the end of his visions, St. John experiences this bridal imagery once more as he sees the new Jerusalem (the People of God, the Church) "coming down out of heaven from God, prepared as a bride adorned for her husband" (21:2).

Saints and mystics, especially Carmelites such as Sts. John of the Cross and Teresa of Ávila, burn with a passion for the soul's bridal relationship with God. In his poem, "Living Flame of Love," John of the Cross aches with desire and wonder. He writes:

O Living Flame of Love / That woundest tenderly / My soul in its inmost depth! / As Thou art no longer grievous / Perfect Thy work, if it be Thy will / Break the web of this sweet encounter.[5]

St. John of the Cross recognizes God's work in his interior depth. God has wounded his soul with his love. Once painful, it becomes sweet. All that remains is the consummation of the soul's encounter with the Bridegroom.

What a sweet marinade to soak in! St. John of the Cross had years to soak in this marinade while sitting in prison. And yet it accomplished precisely God's plan: to lead St. John into a bridal relationship with God himself, to illuminate in the darkness of his prison cell the brightness of spiritual virginity. Oh, that the prisons and darkness of our changed scripts and crushing misfortunes would do the same—that they would be the means for creating more space within us to be totally available for union with God!

I know that spousal union with God and spiritual virginity can be difficult to swallow at first, because it resembles an encounter with some modern art—we can see the shapes but it makes no pattern in our brain. We're so accustomed to thinking of salvation as being "safe" from the fires of hell and of virginity as having to do with sex that connecting God with virginity and our spiritual lives with spousal union feels like a computer virus entering our minds and freezing the processing. It can even be upsetting and disorienting.

However, Jesus said, "I have come to set the earth on fire, and how I wish it were already blazing!" (Luke 12:49). Jesus came to change our categories of thinking, not to preserve the status quo. When Jesus spoke about being one with the Father (see John 17:21), his message completely crossed the wires in the brains of the Jews. They only knew how to think of God in the categories of being One (not Three) and totally transcendent and separate from this earth. And now this Galilean comes along and says there's more than one Person in God and that, in fact, he is God. In his typical fashion, Jesus is asking them to change their categories of thinking (again!).

The same is true for us. We have a category in our minds marked "virgin," and it means "someone who hasn't had sex," and now

I'm asking you, just as the Holy Spirit asked me, to delete that definition and change it to "someone who is totally available for union" and apply it to your relationship with God. Through suffering, detachment, and consecration—through life not going the way we want—God desires not only that we be reconnected to him but that we live in a spousal relationship with him.

But it may take us a while to get there. We expect human love to satisfy our needs for intimacy. We don't see how an invisible God can fulfill the deepest desires of our hearts. And yet this is precisely the "good news" of the gospel. God desires to be not only Lord, Brother, Savior, Friend, Father, and Shepherd but also our Virgin Spouse. And frequently the only way this reality comes crashing into our lives is through disappointment, betrayal, pain, and suffering. God hollows us out so that we cling to him and him alone.

Salvation: United with the Body of Christ

And along the way, even our very definition of salvation changes, which reconfigures the way we think about our ultimate destiny. Instead of salvation being "safe" from the fires of hell or floating around on clouds playing our harps, the Divine Marinade leads us to a different reality: salvation is being totally united to the body of Christ.

When I say, "Salvation is being totally united to the body of Christ," what type of union am I speaking of? A virginal, spousal union, of course! (You knew that was coming, didn't you?) How can our minds possibly grasp the reality of this? Am I just spinning language to make it mean whatever I want?

Obviously, I hope not. What reassures me is that we already experience this spousal and virginal union with God here on earth in the Eucharist. The Catholic Church believes that the bread and wine truly become the body and blood of Christ at every Mass by the power of the Holy Spirit. That means that while the appearance of bread and wine remains, a deeper substantial reality is present: the actual Person of Christ, his body and blood. As a result, when we receive the Eucharist, we are truly one body with Christ. The two, Christ and the Church (each of us), have become one flesh, just as St. Paul proclaimed in Ephesians 5. But please note: while this is truly a bodily union, it is not a sexual union. Rather, it is a virginal union.

Incredible, isn't it? We already live the virginal reality of the body here on earth every time we go to Communion. We already have the privilege of experiencing salvation at every Eucharist, of being united to the body of Christ. The Eucharist rips the veil in two between heaven and earth, and we get a sneak preview of our ultimate destiny—heaven. In Pope John Paul II's words, "The Eucharist is truly a glimpse of heaven appearing on earth. It is a glorious ray of the heavenly Jerusalem which pierces the clouds of our history and lights up our journey."[6]

Ultimately, the reason virginity adds such sweetness to the Divine Marinade is because it's a lightning bolt illuminating heaven. In heaven we will all be virgins! I hope that makes you smile. It makes me grin from ear to ear! And yet, if we understand the full definition of virginity as being totally available for union both physically and spiritually, then virginity reveals our ultimate destiny: to be perfectly united to God forever in both body and spirit.

The great news is that your body is going with you all the way to heaven! Are you jumping up and down for joy? This is great news! Your body is one of your greatest gifts, not one of your greatest burdens. Spousal union can only happen through the body. This is why the unique way spouses express their love to each other, which is different from the way they express themselves to any one else, is through the body, through sexual union. Jesus, at the Last Supper and on the cross, said to us, "This is my body, which will be given for you." He is making a spousal gift of self to us through the body. And as I mentioned before, this spousal gift is offered to us (in a virginal way) every time we receive holy Communion, because God designed us as persons to express our spousal love through the body.

In heaven our ability for spousal love doesn't disappear or become purely spiritual or disembodied. We do not become like angels with a purely spiritual nature and no physical dimension. Instead, we become like Christ in his glorified body. At the end of time, what is referred to as the *eschaton*, Christ will return to earth not as a humble baby but as the victorious King. At that time, when history reaches its consummation, our bodies are raised from the dead, glorified, and perfectly reunited with our spirits (soul) for all eternity.

And here's the encore—we are perfectly united to Christ's glorified body. The perfect union of our glorified body with our purified spirit makes us totally available for union with God. Our heavenly perfection re-creates us as perfect virgins and unites us to Christ's perfectly virginal body. The two, we and God, are one flesh perfectly forever! The Mass is God's own version of "My Space"; he allows us to see on his Eucharistic page the union he anticipates with us for all eternity. What we experience momentarily on earth will be experienced in its totality in heaven. John Paul II reminds us, "Those who feed on Christ in the Eucharist need not wait until the hereafter to receive eternal life: *they already possess it on earth*, as the first-fruits of a future fullness which will embrace man in his totality."[7]

SOAKING IN THE MARINADE

Okay, it's time to go back to the marinade and soak for a while to let these realities become not just abstract concepts but a part of who we are. If you go to prayer and just rest in this thought— a virgin is someone who's totally available for union—I guarantee that you will begin to feel different. You will begin to discover a side of yourself that you didn't know existed, a part of you that is created for total and complete union with God, a part of you that doesn't have to strive to be in God's presence but can rest in

God's presence. You will come to love spiritual virginity and its sweetness in your life, and anticipate the joy of receiving back your virginal body in heaven.

One woman who has discovered the sweetness of spiritual virginity is a dear friend named Judy. Judy is a single mom, marketing consultant, college instructor, and mother of two college-aged children. The script of her life changed abruptly through sexual abuse at a young age. Growing up, guilt and shame became her insistent twin companions.

Judy's marriage ended after nine years. Depression joined guilt and shame as her traveling companions, constantly reinforcing a lack of value and worth set in motion by the abuse.

A week after her son graduated from high school, Judy's father dropped dead on her mother's birthday. It was shocking and devastating. Two months later, her son moved out to go to college. A year and a half later, her daughter decided to move in with her dad for the last few months of her senior year of high school. Judy was consumed with emptiness. Finally, she had to face the ugly truth: the only reason she was living was for her children and not for herself.

Struggling to avoid emotional capsizing, Judy began a twelve-step Christian recovery program called "Celebrate Recovery." There, a new language began to be written on the tablet of her heart, which told her that she mattered to the Lord and had value to him. Slowly, tentatively, she revealed to God and a few friends the fragile corners of her heart where the pain and shame had lodged. Like a crocus encouraged by warm sunshine to poke through the frozen ground, Judy dared to believe that she was the beloved, that she was chosen and loved by God, despite what had been done to her. God even called her by a new name, "lily"—pure and white—and she began to pray for the Lord to "re-virginize" her—to make her totally available for union with him and others.

At first, the thought of being a virgin again seemed as foreign as cheering for the New England Patriots (Judy is a die-hard Pittsburgh Steelers fan). It was hard to imagine her body as pure and virginal rather than a source of abuse, depression, shame, or temptation. However, as she faced one script change after another, Judy experienced an intimacy and hunger for union and communion with God that she never knew could exist on the menu of life.

A major victory occurred on the day she took her daughter shopping for the high school formal. While her daughter was in the changing room, Judy looked in the mirror, and for the first time, she liked what she saw: a woman who mattered to God, who had *feminine* value and worth. Here's how Judy describes her renewed relationship with God:

A few months ago I was getting ready for work. I had a long day ahead of me, and I was packing a lunch and talking to the Lord as I would talk to a friend. In such an intimate way, I heard the Lord say to me, "Honey, I am taking care of everything." In the depths of my heart, I was able to not only hear but also receive the Lord calling me "Honey." I am his honey! It was so endearing. It was like a husband coming down in the morning and saying to his spouse, "Honey, I will take care of it." I just stopped in the midst of what I was doing and said, "Thank you, Lord Jesus."

Through years of hard work, Judy is finally experiencing the honey-like sweetness of the Divine Marinade, of soaking in God's intimate love. She continues the practical work of ruthlessly cutting out whatever undermines the body-spirit connection in order to seek the crystal clear, "five-bar connection" with God all the time—especially by stationing herself as sentinel of her own mind and heart. For example, she tries to select only TV shows and movies that don't lead to victim thinking and other temptations such as lustful thoughts. Her passion for life and for the Lord has returned. She is able to "offer back" her children to God and realize that they belong to him. She is becoming free—free to embrace the outcome of her life, whether "A" or "B" happens, because the Lord is her Spouse, the one she is virginally united to. Facing her script changes with the help of a Christian recovery group allowed Judy to encounter God not only as protector and provider but as her Spouse who intimately loves her.

Detachment, consecration, and spiritual virginity—these are the ingredients of the Divine Marinade that mix together to penetrate into our deepest core. As we allow our heart, emotions, memory—indeed our whole being—to rest in these spiritual realities, we become free to say, "Whatever the outcome, I embrace it with passion." We no longer react to life not going our way by digging in our heels or becoming immobilized, but by constantly offering the situation back to God. We grow in our freedom to be totally available for union with God, to live spiritual virginity as a natural quality of our everyday life. When we do this, we can't help but experience the script changes of life differently, draw in the pure air of spiritual virginity, and eagerly anticipate every Mass as "God's Space" in time and in eternity.

Questions for Reflection and Discussion:

1. What thoughts or ideas struck you in this chapter?

2. What attachments do you have that take up space within you and crowd out God? What's one thing you need to be detached from?

3. Is it frightening to think of giving God more room in your life?

4. What's your reaction to St. Francis' story of perfect joy?

5. Before this chapter, what was your impression of Christian detachment? What is it now?

6. What's something God has asked you to offer back to him? Make a quick list of five things you can consecrate to God in your life now.

7. Have you ever thought of yourself as a spiritual virgin? Is it possible for you to become one?

8. What has the Eucharist meant to you in the past? What does it mean to you now?

If you so desire, take a moment, and ask God to "re-virginize" you. Find a private space (in your home or, if possible, in Eucharistic adoration), and imagine the Holy Spirit descending upon you as you pray. Begin at the top of your head, and work through your whole body, saying, "Holy Spirit, come and re-virginize my mind, come and re-virginize my memory, come and re-virginize my eyes, my mouth, my heart" . . . and continue through your whole body. You may want to pray this prayer daily, weekly, or every time you receive the Eucharist.

Chapter 6

The Body, Suffering, and Love

A group of women in a Bible study were reading the Old Testament book of Malachi. As they studied chapter three, they came across verse three, which says, "He [God] will sit as a refiner and purifier of silver" (RSV). They were puzzled as to what this statement meant about the character and nature of God. One of the women offered to investigate the process of refining silver and get back to the group at the next meeting.

Later that week the woman called up a silversmith and made an appointment to watch him at work. She didn't mention anything about the reason for her interest in silver beyond her curiosity about the refining process. As she watched the silversmith, he held a piece of silver over the fire and allowed it to heat up. He explained that in refining silver, one needed to hold the silver in the middle of the fire where the flames are the hottest so as to burn away all the impurities.

The woman thought about God holding us in such a hot spot. Then she thought again about how God is a refiner and purifier of silver. She asked the silversmith if it was true that he had to sit there in front of the fire the whole time the silver was being refined. The man answered that he not only had to sit there holding the silver, but he had to keep his eyes on the silver the entire time it was in the fire. If the silver was left even a moment too long in the flames, it would be destroyed. The woman was silent for a moment. Then she asked the silversmith, "How do you know when the silver is fully refined?" He smiled at her and answered, "Oh, that's easy—when I see my image in it."[1]

The reflections in this book have considered various ways of being in the "hot spot"—of how we are purified by such things as alcoholism, anorexia, accidents, loneliness, illness, infertility, family relationships, children leaving the nest, and divorce. Do we ever think about how the process can refine us into God's image? This can be a bit tricky because *direct evil is never willed by God*. Sexual abuse, for example, is *not* God's way of refining us into his image. And yet, if we allow him, God's divine mercy can use the heat of our trials and sufferings for a noble purpose, for refashioning us into his image and likeness.

The Meaning and Purpose of the Body

This brings us to the wonderful topic of the body. What is the meaning and purpose of the body? Is it simply to lug around until we finally shed it like a snakeskin? Quite the contrary. We are made in God's image and likeness precisely because, as human persons, we are created of body and spirit. We image God, not by being like angels (purely spiritual), nor by being like animals (purely physical), but through a unique combination of the two. We are embodied spirits, incarnated souls. To be a human person means to image God by being both body and spirit.

It also means that we are in a unique and unrepeatable relationship with God. Genesis 1:27 says, "God created man in his image; in the divine image he created him; male and female he created them." From the moment of our conception, we come into being in relationship with God. This is our origin.

But we also have a destiny. Our destiny is to be united to God forever—to transcend the material world as we know it and to live eternally in the presence of God. However, our ultimate destiny is not purely a spiritual one, as the last chapter reminded us. Our physical bodies are also destined to transcend this earth and to be raised in a glorified manner and united with God.

Sometimes I think we forget how utterly radical the resurrection of the body is. For the Greek and Roman cultures that surrounded the Jews at the time of Jesus' birth and death, the body was considered a prison, something that entrapped the soul. "Salvation" was the liberation of the soul from the body; it was a purely spiritual state. Jesus' resurrection radically opposes this view of salvation. In his glorified body, Jesus reveals the goodness of creation, the goodness of the body, and the goodness of our embodied human nature. Therefore, the goal of every human life is the perfect integration of body and spirit, not the shedding of the body to "free" the spirit. And in a mysterious way, suffering plays a key role in this integration.

It almost sounds as if I'm contradicting myself, doesn't it?

Precisely when we suffer in body (a physical suffering) or in spirit (a mental or emotional suffering), we usually feel a pull, an interior disruption between body and spirit, not a deeper integration. How can suffering accomplish the latter?

BACK TO THE BEGINNING

In his apostolic letter entitled "On the Christian Meaning of Human Suffering," Pope John Paul II addressed this issue. He said, "Suffering seems to belong to man's transcendence: it is one of those points in which man is in a certain sense 'destined' to go beyond himself, and he is called to this in a mysterious way."[2] Suffering, as my introduction to this book noted, prompts us to ask, "Why?" This is a particularly human question, one not asked by the animals. John Paul II writes, "Man can put this question to God with all the emotion of his heart and with his mind full of dismay and anxiety; and God expects the question and listens to it. "[3]

What does suffering do? It provokes us to go beyond ourselves, to transcend ourselves and the physical reality we can see. Suffering, if we allow it, will take us back "to the beginning," back to our origin in God. The suffering in our body, whether it is physical or emotional, can become the place of communion with God.[4]

Oh, what a grace to have a body that can suffer and a mind that can ask why! In a very human way, God allows and invites us to rediscover the foundational truth of our existence: God as our Father and Creator (first a daughter, then a bride!). It sounds so simple, almost childish, and yet when we are grieving a profound loss, such as the loss of a spouse, child, job, relationship, dream, economic security, or our health, sometimes the last thing we want to do is acknowledge God's fatherhood and sovereignty. We want to be angry; we want the situation to change; we want to take things into our own hands; we want science and technology to be our salvation.

Finally, when we have exhausted our options, or have cycled through the stages of grief (denial, anger, bargaining, depression, and acceptance)[5] for the tenth time, we encounter again, or perhaps for the first time, God's fatherhood in our own life. The hand that has tightly clutched the control of our life begins to release. Deep within our being, an identity shift begins to take place: God as the Origin and Giver of life takes root within us. This is what I like to call the "sunflower moment" in our lives.

With Our Bodies, We Relate to Others

Years ago, as I was traveling across France by train, we passed fields and fields of sunflowers with their cheerful faces all turned the same direction. Before this moment, I had never realized that a sunflower is so named because it follows the sun: in the morning, all the flowers face east, and as the sun tracks across the sky, so also the sunflowers follow the movement of the sun. Suffering, if we allow it, can orient us in the same way so that our interior being tracks the presence of God throughout the day. We acknowledge God as Origin, Source, Original Giver, and Father. We encounter God constantly in the garden of our soul, just as Adam and Eve did before the Fall, and we know indelibly that he is the origin and destiny of our life. Our existence is God's gift, not our own doing.[6]

And all this has happened through the body. The suffering in our bodies leads us to our dignity as daughters (and sons) of the Father. It reconnects us, so to speak, with the breath of life within us, with God's Spirit within us. We begin to glimpse that the body is not just a "body," but the meeting point between flesh and spirit—our human spirit and God's Spirit. The body is the stage where the dramatic relationship between God and us is played out. The body, united with the spirit, creates in us the capacity to relate to God and others. It is the place of relationship, of communion.[7]

Not only does suffering invite us "back" to our origin in God, it also invites us to plumb the depths of love. Continuing his reflections on the "why" question, John Paul II says: "But in order to perceive the true answer to the 'why' of suffering, we must look to the revelation of divine love, the ultimate source of the meaning of everything that exists. Love is also the richest source of the meaning of suffering." [8]

While we are often tempted to divorce love from suffering ("If God really loved me, I wouldn't have to suffer . . ."), John Paul II does the opposite. Suffering, and indeed the meaning of our lives, remains incomprehensible without love. "Love," John Paul II says, "is also the fullest source of the answer to the question of the meaning of suffering. This answer has been given by God to man in the Cross of Jesus Christ."[9]

Why do you suffer, or why does your child, parent, spouse, or friend suffer? The answer lies hidden in the cross of Christ. Divine Love is not only paternal love (fatherly love), it is also salvific love: "For God so loved the world that he gave his only Son, so that everyone who believes in him might not perish but might have eternal life" (John 3:16).

Salvation is an eternal communion of love with God in the perfection of our personhood, both body and spirit. Salvific love, therefore, overcomes the loss of eternal communion with God; it overcomes the dominion of sin and death. God the Father "gives" his Son in human history in order to strike at the very roots of human evil.[10] And this "giving" happens through suffering, through the cross.

Here's how John Paul II connects the overcoming of evil with love and the cross: "Precisely by means of his Cross he must strike at the roots of evil, planted in the history of man and in human souls. Precisely by means of his Cross he must accomplish *the work of salvation*. This work, in the plan of eternal Love, has a redemptive character."[11]

LOVE UNLEASHED!

We are back to God changing our categories of thinking. The tragic consequence of sin is the loss of being able to express love properly through our bodies.[12] Our ruptured relationship with God creates a rupture within us between body and spirit, which spills over into fractured relationships with others. Death is the ultimate expression of all these ruptures, which is why we experience it as the wrenching that it is—the unnatural separation of the body and the spirit, and the body from those we love.

Christ, however, conquers death by death; he robs suffering of its power to take us away from Love and those we love precisely by suffering with love. Or as John Paul II says: "Christ goes toward his own suffering, aware of its saving power. He goes forward in obedience to the Father, but primarily he is *united to the Father in this love* with which he has loved the world and man in the world."[13]

Christ refused to allow suffering to separate him from the Father. In the garden of Gethsemane, he earnestly prayed for his suffering to be removed, and yet his final words were "Father . . . not my will but yours be done" (Luke 22:42). In other words, "United to you, Father, I can embrace this suffering, I can embrace my cross." Rather than rupturing his relationship with the Father, Christ's suffering in his body becomes the place of communion with the Father. And, inconceivably, his broken body becomes the place of communion with us: "This is my body given for you."

In short, Christ's body is not only the place of communion with the Father, but through the offering of his body for us, it becomes a place of communion with us and others. Suffering leads not to abandoned isolation but to self-gift in compassion and solidarity. Christ was broken to be given. Likewise, we are broken to be given. Or as John Paul II says, "Suffering, which is present under so many different forms in our human world, is also present in order *to unleash love in the human person*, that unselfish gift of one's 'I' on behalf of other people, especially those who suffer."[14]

Suffering is present to unleash love in us! John Paul II not only talked the talk, but he walked the walk. On May 13, 1981, Turkish gunman Mehmet Ali Agca attempted to put a bullet through John Paul II's heart. He missed, just barely. John Paul II's recovery was slow and painful. However, he allowed this suffering to unleash love in him so that when he was fit and able, he visited Mehmet Ali Agca in prison, embraced him, forgave him, and loved him.

Here's another example. Rachel Muha faced every mother's nightmare: the murder of her joyous eighteen-year-old son, Brian. Brian and his roommate, Aaron, were abducted from their rented apartment, driven to the hills outside of town, and killed. At the murder trial, Rachel looked at the murderer with love and forgiveness and said calmly: "If you hadn't done this, I would have my Brian and you would have your freedom. . . . But losing your freedom is not as bad as losing your soul." She then asked him to redeem the rest of his years on earth before blessing him and assuring him that she would pray for him.[15]

Rachel allowed this suffering to unleash love, not hatred and revenge, in her with the hope it would unleash love in others.

The Web site dedicated to her son (brianmuhafoundation.com) is filled with the spirit of communion and peace. The link entitled "Pray with Us" implores visitors to the site to pray the Divine Mercy Chaplet for Brian's killers:

> How we wish we could just concentrate on his [Brian's] happiness and on doing good works in his memory. But thoughts of Brian bring thoughts of his killers and the eternal misery they face if they don't turn to God.
>
> We are asking you to please pray the Divine Mercy Chaplet as often as you can, for Brian's and Aaron's killers. . . . Their conversion is very important to Brian and Aaron so let's help them attain this miracle—and a miracle it would be! God has given us an enormous task, but not an impossible one.[16]

The blessing of suffering is that we can freely choose to transform our own suffering into love and self-gift. Suffering, through its work of detachment, consecration, faith, hope, and love, doesn't leave the body behind but welds a greater cooperation, a greater harmony, between body and spirit so that the body becomes transparent to the Spirit—and to Love.

Again we see this truth of transparency in the lived experience of Pope John Paul II. As he aged and his body was ravaged by disease, he didn't withdraw his gift of self. He chose to transform his own suffering into a form of love, into the visible expression of self-gift—as he stood at the altar offering the holy Sacrifice of the Mass with saliva trickling down his chin and shaking hands; as he continued to travel hunched over and bearing his aging body on a cane; as he kept up his challenging Christmas schedule, even though eternal rest was indeed just a few months away.

Love, according to John Paul II, became manifested through the body, the suffering body, just as Love was manifested on the cross through the suffering body of Christ. Through Christ's passion, human suffering entered a completely new order by being linked to divine mercy, to "that love which creates good, drawing it out by means of suffering, just as the supreme good of the Redemption of the world was drawn from the Cross of Christ," in the words of John Paul.[17]

Not only have our lives been redeemed, but suffering has been redeemed as well. It is no longer purely the domain of evil. In bringing about redemption through suffering, John Paul II reminds us that "Christ *has* also raised *human suffering to the level of the Redemption*. Thus each man, in his suffering, can also become a sharer in the redemptive suffering of Christ."[18] Or as he put it another way, "Suffering must serve *for conversion*, that is, *for the rebuilding of goodness* in the subject." [19]

SUFFERING REDEEMED

St. Paul graphically describes this state of redeemed suffering: "We are afflicted in every way, but not constrained; perplexed, but not driven to despair; persecuted, but not abandoned; struck down, but not destroyed; always carrying about in the body the dying of Jesus, so that the life of Jesus may also be manifested in our body" (2 Corinthians 4:8-10).

Suffering, if we allow it, can refine God's image in us so that Jesus is revealed through our bodies, even our suffering bodies! How often have we heard the following words from Scripture, and yet they take on new meaning and significance when we are living the paschal mystery through pain and suffering: "I have been crucified with Christ; yet I live, no longer I, but Christ lives in me; insofar as I now live in the flesh, I live by faith in the Son of God who has loved me and given himself up for me" (Galatians 2:19-20).

If we are pliable enough, suffering pushes us to the edge of faith, and then we soar. Once again we soar because the cross is not the end of the story but the gateway to the resurrection of the body. Jesus' risen and glorified body is what allows us to say: "I consider that the sufferings of this present time are as nothing compared with the glory to be revealed for us" (Romans 8:18).

What is this glory? Glory is the visible manifestation of God's presence. Thus, salvific suffering leads to glory—to God being visibly manifested in us. When we suffer, John Paul II says, we become particularly susceptible, particularly open, to the working of the salvific powers of God, offered to humanity through Christ.[20]

What do these salvific powers accomplish? Union! Salvific suffering can actually increase the union between body and spirit because it overcomes the disruptive effects of sin in our lives, and this increases our ability to be in union with God and others.

THE SOURCE OF OUR HOPE

The resurrection of the body, then, becomes the source of our hope. Why? Because it testifies to our *future* glory at work in our bodies, even now. In his ever-realistic style, Pope Benedict XVI begins his encyclical on hope, *Spe Salvi*, with this reminder: "The present, even if it is arduous, can be lived and accepted if it leads toward a goal, if we can be sure of this goal, and if this goal is great enough to justify the effort of the journey."[21]

What is the goal that can sustain us through any trial, any suffering, any wrenching situation? The promise of eternal union with God in our glorified bodies. The distinguishing mark of Christians, Benedict says, is the fact that they have a future: "It is not that they know the details of what awaits them, but they know in general terms that their life will not end in emptiness. Only when the future is certain as a positive reality does it become possible to live the present as well."[22]

Suffering claws at your future and your hope—trying to strip away your confidence in a God who is good . . . all the time, who is working . . . all the time, who is with you . . . all the time. It can reduce your vision, your hope, to only what this world offers; it can strip away your transcendence and convince you that death is the final word, and it is to be feared. The frequently quoted

Psalm 23 that describes the Lord as our shepherd reassures us: "Even when I walk through a dark valley, I fear no harm for you are at my side" (verse 4).

Jesus shows us the way beyond the dark valley and death as the true shepherd. Pope Benedict XVI draws on this image when he writes: "The true shepherd is one who knows even the path that passes through the valley of death; one who walks with me even on the path of final solitude, where no one can accompany me, guiding me through: he himself has walked this path, he has descended into the kingdom of death, he has conquered death, and he has returned to accompany us now and to give us the certainty that, together with him, we can find a way through."[23]

You can find a way through! You can find a way through the pain, uncertainty, despair, and yes, even death, accompanied by Christ. And God willing, like Peter after he had betrayed Christ, you can turn and strengthen your brothers, sisters, neighbors, friends, co-workers, and children. In doing so, you unleash hope in others by maintaining the conviction that suffering will not get the better of you, that it will not deprive you of your dignity and destiny,[24] that it will not separate you from God or others. How many times do we need to hear Romans 8:38-39: "For I am convinced that neither death, nor life, nor angels, nor principalities, nor present things, nor future things, nor powers, nor height, nor depth, nor any other creature will be able to separate us from the love of God in Christ Jesus our Lord."

Suffering, on the contrary, provides the opportunity to rediscover our dignity and destiny, to embrace our body-spirit humanity and our relatedness to God more completely. Even more, we are invited to be cooperators with God in the work of redemption. St. Paul's statement from Colossians 1:24 makes this bold claim: "Now I rejoice in my sufferings for your sake, and in my flesh I am filling up what is lacking in the afflictions of Christ on behalf of his body, which is the church."

How can we possibly "make up" for what is lacking in Christ's sufferings? We can't. Christ's redemptive act is perfect. There is nothing that we add to it. But it is also timeless. That means Christ's redemptive love is waiting to be "completed" in each generation—indeed, in each person. We "complete" Christ's redemptive act when we enter into an everlasting relationship of love with Christ. We also "complete" the sufferings of Christ when we allow suffering to manifest God's love through us to others.

Rachel Muha is "completing" in her flesh, in her life experience (and asking others to join her), what is incomplete in Christ's afflictions—the conversion of her son's murderers. Jesus Christ died for those murderers, and yet his sufferings are incomplete until they participate in them, until they come to a saving relationship of love with Jesus Christ. When the redemption accomplished by Christ "lives on" in us for the sake of the body, for the sake of others' redemption—like Rachel Muha, like John Paul II, like Mother Teresa—then we become the body of Christ, the crucified and broken body from whose side God's life flows to others.

The discovery of the salvific meaning of suffering in union with Christ, John Paul II says, transforms our depressed feelings. "Faith in sharing in the suffering of Christ brings with it the interior certainty that the suffering person 'completes what is lacking in Christ's afflictions'; the certainty that in the spiritual dimension of the work of Redemption *he is serving*, like Christ, *the salvation of his brothers and sisters.*"[25]

This sense of purpose, even if the human situation doesn't change, overcomes the sense of the uselessness of suffering and can even spring forth as a source of joy: "Now I rejoice in my sufferings for your sake. . . ." (Colossians 1:24).

A number of years ago, I composed a simple prayer to help my son and me offer up our sufferings for others. It's a great "ace in the hole" to mentally recite when you slice a finger (I've done that), bang a shin (how many times!), or receive an emotional blow (and your mind goes blank). You may want to adopt it for yourself or your family: "O Jesus, this is for love of you, for the conversion of sinners, for the release of souls from purgatory, and in reparation for sins against the Immaculate Heart of Mary and the Sacred Heart of Jesus."

Benedict XVI also echoes the interconnectedness of our human and spiritual lives, and our ability to be vessels of salvation and hope for others:

No one lives alone. No one sins alone. No one is saved alone. The lives of others continually spill over into mine:

in what I think, say, do and achieve. And conversely, my life spills over into that of others. . . . So my prayer for another is not something extraneous to that person, something external, not even after death. In the interconnectedness of Being, my gratitude to the other—my prayer for him—can play a small part in his purification. . . . It is never too late to touch the heart of another, nor is it ever vain. . . . As Christians we should never limit ourselves to asking: how can I save myself? We should also ask: what can I do in order that others may be saved and that for them too the star of hope may rise? Then I will have done my utmost for my own personal salvation as well.[26]

TURNING SUFFERING INTO LOVE

In his greatest moments of suffering, St. Paul, like Jesus, sought to turn his sufferings into love. As Pope Benedict exhorted, Paul sought to turn his suffering into a means of salvation for others and the world. Oh, that we would be imitators of him as he was an imitator of Christ! Oh, that we would seek to eliminate the presence of suffering and evil in the world, using every possible human means, and yet not shirk our own cross! "It is not by sidestepping or fleeing from suffering that we are healed," Pope Benedict courageously writes, "but rather by our capacity for accepting it, maturing through it and finding meaning *through union with Christ*, who suffered with infinite love."[27]

The full blossoming of mature love into salvific love is the ultimate goal of life, suffering, and even St. Francis' perfect joy. John Paul II reminds us,

> Gradually, *as the individual takes up his cross*, spiritually uniting himself to the cross of Christ, the salvific meaning of suffering is revealed before him. He does not discover this meaning at his own human level, but at the level of the suffering of Christ. At the same time, however, from this level of Christ the salvific meaning of suffering *descends to man's level* and becomes, in a sense, the individual's personal response. It is then that man finds in his suffering interior peace and even spiritual joy.[28]

For most of us, grasping the salvific meaning of suffering doesn't come in a tequila shot but is more like recognizing a fine, aged wine: after repeatedly tasting suffering, we begin to have a more discriminating palate that recognizes the more subtle layers of its meaning. We begin to see the connection between suffering and love, and are willing to drink of the paschal cup, even if only in small, initial sips. Then, we begin to say with fear and trembling, "I am crucified with Christ. . . ."

Questions for Reflection and Discussion:

1. Take a moment to review this chapter. What thoughts or ideas were new to you? Did anything make you feel uncomfortable?

2. Discuss how suffering can remind us of our origin.

3. What is the purpose of suffering *in the body*?

4. What does it mean to join our sufferings to Christ's sufferings on the cross?

5. If you were in Rachel Muha's shoes, what would you have done?

6. What are your thoughts on this quote: "Suffering, which is present under so many different forms in our human world, is also present in order *to unleash love in the human person*"? Have you experienced this in your own life or in someone else's life?

7. What do you think Pope Benedict means by the following: "Suffering and torment is still terrible and well-nigh unbearable. Yet the star of hope has risen—the anchor of the heart reaches the very throne of God. Instead of evil being unleashed

within man, the light shines victorious: suffering—without ceasing to be suffering—becomes, despite everything, a hymn of praise"? (*Spe Salvi*, 37)

8. Take a moment and pray to be united to Christ's sufferings on the cross and join your greatest present suffering(s) to his.

CHAPTER 7

A FINAL CUP OF TEA

If you made it through the last chapter, I congratulate you! And I apologize. Trying to condense my thoughts on one of the most contested topics in Christianity (how we "make up" for Christ's sufferings in our own bodies) is like trying to contain a full batch of popcorn in a little saucepan: the kernels keep popping out everywhere, despite your best effort to keep the lid secured.

Of course, there's no absolute, secure answer to the question of evil and suffering. There will always be erratic popcorn kernels that fly here and there, despite our best efforts to contain them in the neat categories of our minds. I would be styling myself as an alternate god if I maintained I had the one answer to pain and suffering. Instead, I have tried to offer perspectives to help bring meaning and purpose out of life when it doesn't go your way so as to lead you to a deeper life of faith, hope, and ultimately love—spousal and salvific love.

I'd like to end this book with a final reflection on the journey of life—on those times when we feel clobbered, pinched, overwhelmed, and ready to give up. You may or may not be familiar with this story. In either case, I ask you to read it and then ponder it as your journey to becoming all that God intended for you, from "the beginning."

May you know your true beauty, one that comes from Christ's light shining within you as well as the goodness of your body—yes *your* body—in all its feminine hormonal shifts, emotional ups and down, and relational roller coasters. **You are loved, you are the beloved, and you are beautiful.**

There was a couple who used to go to England to shop. They both liked antiques and pottery, and especially teacups. This was their twenty-fifth wedding anniversary.

One day in a beautiful shop they saw a beautiful teacup. They said to the sales clerk, "May we see that teacup? We've never seen one quite so beautiful." As the clerk handed the teacup to the couple, the teacup began to speak.

"I haven't always been a teacup. There was a time when I was red and I was clay. My master took me and rolled me and patted me over and over, and I yelled out, 'Let me alone,' but he only smiled and said, 'Not yet.'

"Then I was placed on a spinning wheel," the teacup continued, "and suddenly I was spun around and around and around. 'Stop it! I'm getting dizzy!' I screamed. But the master only smiled and said, 'Not yet.'

"Then he put me in the oven. I never felt such heat. I wondered why he wanted to burn me, and I yelled and knocked at the door. I could see him through the opening and I could read his lips as he shook his head, 'Not yet.'

"Finally the door opened, he put me on the shelf, and I

began to cool. 'There, that's better,' I said. And he brushed and painted me all over. The fumes were horrible. I thought I would gag. 'Stop it, stop it!' I cried. He only nodded, 'Not yet.'

"Then suddenly he put me back into the oven, not like the first one. This one was twice as hot, and I knew I would suffocate. I begged. I pleaded. I screamed. I cried. All the time I could see him through the window, shaking his head and saying, 'Not yet.'

"Then I knew there was no hope. I would never make it. I was ready to give up. But the door opened, and he took me out and placed me on the shelf. One hour later he handed me a mirror and said, 'Look at yourself.' And I did. I said, 'That's not me; that couldn't be me. It's beautiful. I'm beautiful.'

"Then my master said to me, 'I want you to remember that I know it hurt to be rolled and patted, but if I had left you alone, you would have dried up. I know it made you dizzy to spin around on the wheel, but if I had stopped, you would have crumbled. I know it was hot and disagreeable in the oven, but if I hadn't put you there, you would have cracked. I know the fumes were bad when I brushed and painted you all over, but if I hadn't done that, you never would have hardened; you would not have had any color in your life. And if I hadn't put you back in that second oven, you wouldn't have survived for very long, because you needed to become harder still. Now you are finished. You are what I had in mind when I first began with you.'"[1]

Questions for Reflection and Discussion:

1. What are your thoughts on the teacup story?

2. Do you identify with any stage of the teacup in particular?

3. When you look in the mirror, what do you see? Are you able to see yourself as beautiful?

4. How have your thoughts on pain and suffering changed over the course of this book?

5. If you could ask God one question about anything, what would it be?

6. If you are meeting in a group, tell the group one thing you would like them to pray for. If you have the time, go around the group and have each person pray for the person on their left for that person's special intention.

Do you have a story you'd like to share with Katrina? If so, please email her at Katrina@wttm.org.

Sources and Acknowledgments

Chapter 1: The Goodness of God

1. The title of this story is "The Ivory and Gold Tablecloth" by Howard C. Schade. It originally appeared in *Reader's Digest* in 1954. There is a similar, modern version that is very popular on the Internet. For more information, see snopes.com/glurge /tablecloth.asp.

2. St. Augustine, Sermon 88.5.

Chapter 2: The Script Changes . . . Unexpectedly

1. http://www.gcfl.net/archive.php?funny=19990312, submitted by Rosemary Jett.

2. http://www.gcfl.net/archive.php?funny=19990831,submitted by Erma Lee McMinn.

3. http://www.gcfl.net/archive.php?funny=19990709, submitted by William Oswald.

4. Here's an article summarizing James Berger's heroism: talk.livedaily.com/archive/index.php/t-133597.html.

Chapter 3: The Way of the Cross

1. Fr. Henri Nouwen, *The Path of Waiting* (New York: Crossroads, 1995), 16–17.

2. Fr. Henri Nouwen, 15.

3. Fr. Henri Nouwen, 15.

4. Fr. Henri Nouwen, 19.

5. Fr. Henri Nouwen, 13.

6. For a list of biblical promises, see biblicalstudies.ozwide.net.au /bible_promises.html.

7. Fr. Henri Nouwen, 22.

8. "Life Issues Connector," February 2004, 2; true story shared by Dr. John Wilke about another medical doctor. Used with permission.

9. This story was told in a homily given by Cardinal Sean O'Malley on his blog posted on August 17, 2007, and can be accessed at: cardinalseansblog.org/?m=2007/08/17.

10. Translation is from the New American Bible, 1970 edition.

CHAPTER 4: THE EUCHARISTIC PATTERN

1. John Paul II, Encyclical Letter *Ecclesia de Eucharistica,* April 17, 2003, no. 20, accessed at vatican.va.

2. Translation is from the New American Bible, 1970 edition.

3. Fr. Henri Nouwen, *Life of the Beloved* (New York: Crossroads, 1997), 41–42.

4. Fr. Henri Nouwen, 45.

5. Fr. Henri Nouwen, 59.

6. See morrismn.info/nunandvietnam.htm for the full story.

7. Fr. Henri Nouwen, 62.

8. Fr. Henri Nouwen, 62–63.

9. Fr. Henri Nouwen, 71.

10. Fr. Henri Nouwen, 79.

11. This story appears to be similar to the one told in *The Pumpkin Patch Parable* by Liz Curtis Higgs. See lizcurtishiggs.com/nelson /pumpkin.htm.

12. cf. John Paul II, Encyclical Letter *Dives in Misericordia,* "The Mercy of God," November 30, 1980, no. 7, accessed at vatican.va.

13. John Paul II, "The Mercy of God," no. 6.

14. cf. Fr. Henri Nouwen, *The Path of Waiting*, 20.

15. Author unknown. This story, known as "The Cracked Pot" is posted on various Web sites. See state.sc.us/dmh/bryan/wbful .htm for one of the postings.

16. Mark Schultz, "Broken and Beautiful," on the CD entitled *Broken and Beautiful*, available from markschultzmusic.com.

17. Fr. Henri Nouwen, *Life of the Beloved*, 82–83.

18. Fr. Henri Nouwen, 92.

CHAPTER 5: THE DIVINE MARINADE

1. Fr. Iain Matthew, *Impact of God: Soundings from St. John of the Cross* (London: Hodder and Stoughton, 1995), 35.

2. Fr. Iain Matthew, 37.

3. Brother Leo Ugolino, *The Little Flowers of St. Francis of Assisi* (New York: Random House, 1998), Chapter VIII; available online at ccel.org/ccel/ugolino/flowers.iii.viii.html.

4. These reflections on union and fruitfulness in God led me to understand in a new way the Catholic Church's teaching on contraception. The Catholic Church has always taught—and continues to teach despite very vocal objections—that contraception violates God's design. Marital union is designed by God to be a mirror of (and, dare I say it, a participation in) the inner life of the Trinity—to be both unitive and fruitful. However, a contraceptive act of intercourse intentionally removes the fruitfulness of the marital act. Thus, it changes the very image of God from a fruitful Trinity to a sterile duality. In short, contraception says there is no Holy Spirit and that God's love is self-contained rather than overflowing. For more on this, see my article posted online at ccli.org/ resources/pub/CCLFamilyFoundations2004-1112.pdf.

5. St. John of the Cross, *The Dark Night of the Soul & the Living Flame of Love* (London: HarperCollins, 1995), 162.

6. John Paul II, Encyclical Letter *Ecclesia de Eucharistica,* April 17, 2003, no. 19, accessed at vatican.va.

7. John Paul II, no. 18.

Chapter 6: The Body, Suffering, and Love

1. Author unknown. This story circulates on the Internet in various forms. For one example see scborromeo.org/wisdom/malachi33.htm.

2. John Paul II, Apostolic Letter *Salvifici Doloris,* "On the Christian Meaning of Human Suffering," February 11, 1984, no. 2, accessed at vatican.va.

3. John Paul II, no. 10.

4. Many thoughts in this chapter are culled from Fr. José Granados' article, "Toward a Theology of the Suffering Body" in *Communio: International Catholic Review*, 33 (Winter 2006), 540–563.

5. These stages can be found in Elisabeth Kübler-Ross, *On Death and Dying* (New York: Touchstone, 1969).

6. See Fr. José Granados, 561.

7. Fr. Granados says, "The body appears as the place of communion between God and man and between man and woman" (542).

8. John Paul II, no. 13.

9. John Paul II, no. 13.

10. See John Paul II, no. 15.

11. John Paul II, no. 16.

12. See Fr. José Granados, 544–545.

13. John Paul II, no. 16.

14. John Paul II, no. 29.

15. Mrs. Muha is quoted by Tony Norman in his Pittsburgh Post-Gazette column of September 1, 2000, accessed at post-gazette.com/columnists/20000901tony.asp.

16. See brianmuhafoundation.com/Prayer.html.

17. John Paul II, no. 18.

18. John Paul II, no. 19.

19. John Paul II, no. 12.

20. See John Paul II, no. 23.

21. Benedict XVI, Encyclical Letter *Spe Salvi*, "In Hope We Were Saved," November 30, 2007, no. 1, accessed at vatican.va.

22. Benedict XVI, no. 2.

23. Benedict XVI, no. 6.

24. See John Paul II, no. 23.

25. John Paul II, no. 27.

26. Benedict XVI, no. 48.

27. Benedict XVI, no. 37, emphasis added.

28. John Paul II, no. 26.

Chapter 7: A Final Cup of Tea

1. Author unknown. This story circulates on the Internet in various forms. For one posting, see all-creatures.org/stories/teacup.html.